The Rape of Childhood

Margaret S. Mahler Series

This series of yearly volumes began appearing in 1991, and is based upon the panel discussions presented at the prestigious Annual Margaret Mahler Symposia held in Philadelphia. Each volume consists of three papers and their discussions presented at the most recent Symposium. A thorough introduction and a comprehensive conclusion that pulls all the material together are specially written for the book. Occasionally, one or two papers that were not presented at the meeting but represent the cutting-edge thinking on the topic are also included. While this format and organization gives these books a friendly familiarity, the books' contents vary greatly and are invariably a source of excitement and clinical enthusiasm. Volumes published so far have addressed topics as diverse as hatred and cultural differences in childhood development, extramarital affairs and sibling relationship, mourning and self psychology, and resilience and boundary violations. Among the distinguished psychoanalysts whose work has appeared in this series are Salman Akhtar, Anni Bergman, Harold Blum, Ruth Fischer, Alvin Frank, Dorothy Holmes, Otto Kernberg, Selma Kramer, Peter Neubauer, Henri Parens, Fred Pine, John Munder Ross, and Ernest Wolf, to name a few. The vantage point is always broad-based and includes developmental, clinical, and cultural variables but the end point is consistently an enhancement of the technical armamentarium of the therapist.

BOOKS BASED UPON THE MARGARET S. MAHLER SYMPOSIA

Thicker Than Blood: Bonds of Fantasy and Reality in Adoption (1999), by Salman Akhtar and Selma Kramer

Does God Help? Developmental and Clinical Aspects of Religious Belief (2000), edited by Salman Akhtar and Henri Parens

Three Faces of Mourning: Melancholia, Manic Defense, and Moving On (2001), edited by Salman Akhtar

Real and Imaginary Fathers: Development, Transference, and Healing (2004), edited by Salman Akhtar and Henri Parens

The Language of Emotions: Developmental, Psychopathology, and Technique (2005), edited by Salman Akhtar and Harold P. Blum

Interpersonal Boundaries: Variations and Violations (2006), edited by Salman Akhtar

Listening to Others: Developmental and Clinical Aspects of Empathy and Attunement (2007), edited by Salman Akhtar

The Unbroken Soul: Tragedy, Trauma, and Human Resilience (2008), edited by Henri Parens, Harold P. Blum, Salman Akhtar

Lying, Cheating, and Carrying On: Developmental, Clinical, and Sociocultural Aspects of Dishonesty and Deceit (2009), by Salman Akhtar and Henri Parens

The Electrified Mind: Development, Psychopathology, and Treatment in the Era of Cell Phones and the Internet (2011), edited by Salman Akhtar

The Mother and Her Child: Clinical Aspects of Attachment, Separation, and Loss (2012), edited by Salman Akhtar

Guilt: Origins, Manifestations, and Management (2013), edited by Salman Akhtar

Human Goodness: Origins, Manifestations, and Management (2014), edited by Salman Akhtar

The New Motherhoods: Patterns of Early Child Care in Contemporary Culture (2015), edited by Salman Akhtar

Divorce: Emotional Impact and Therapeutic Interventions (2016), edited by Salman Akhtar

Before and After Violence (2017), edited by Salman Akhtar

The Rape of Childhood: Developmental, Clinical, and Sociocultural Aspects of Childhood Sexual Abuse (2019), edited by Salman Akhtar

The Rape of Childhood

Developmental, Clinical, and Sociocultural Aspects of Childhood Sexual Abuse

Edited by Salman Akhtar

LEXINGTON BOOKS
Lanham • Boulder • New York • London

Published by Lexington Books
An imprint of The Rowman & Littlefield Publishing Group, Inc.
4501 Forbes Boulevard, Suite 200, Lanham, Maryland 20706
www.rowman.com

Unit A, Whitacre Mews, 26-34 Stannary Street, London SE11 4AB

British Library Cataloguing in Publication Information Available

Library of Congress Cataloging-in-Publication Data

Names: Margaret S. Mahler Symposium on Child Development (49th : 2018 : Philadelphia, Pa.), author. | Akhtar, Salman, 1946 July 31- editor.
Title: The rape of childhood : developmental, clinical, and sociocultural aspects of childhood sexual abuse / edited by Salman Akhtar.
Description: : Lanham : Lexington Books, [2018] | Series: Margaret S. Mahler series | Based upon Margaret S. Mahler symposium. | Includes bibliographical references and index.
Identifiers: LCCN 2018038545 (print) | LCCN 2018039073 (ebook) | ISBN 9781498587846 (Electronic) | ISBN 9781498587839 (cloth : alk. paper)
Subjects: | MESH: Child Abuse, Sexual--psychology | Child Abuse, Sexual--therapy | Adult Survivors of Child Abuse--psychology | Congresses
Classification: LCC RJ507.S49 (ebook) | LCC RJ507.S49 (print) | NLM WS 350 | DDC 616.85/8360651--dc23
LC record available at https://lccn.loc.gov/2018038545

∞™ The paper used in this publication meets the minimum requirements of American National Standard for Information Sciences Permanence of Paper for Printed Library Materials, ANSI/NISO Z39.48-1992.

Printed in the United States of America

To the memory of
Margaret S. Mahler and Selma Kramer

Contents

Acknowledgments

All the chapters in this book, except chapters 1 and 8, were originally presented as papers at the 49th Annual Margaret S. Mahler Symposium on Child Development, held on April 21, 2018. We wish to express gratitude to the Department of Psychiatry of Jefferson Medical College, the main sponsor of this event. We are especially indebted to Dr. Michael Vergare, chairman of the Department of Psychiatry and Human Behavior of the Jefferson Medical College, Mary Etezady, chair of the Board of the Psychoanalytic Foundation of the Psychoanalytic Center of Philadelphia, and William Singletary, president of the Margaret S. Mahler Foundation for their continued kind support. On behalf of Dr. Calvin Colarusso, one of the contributors to this book, we express our gratitude to Dr. Gordon Caras, for providing a meaningful addendum to Dr. Colarusso's chapter. There are many others who helped in subtle and not-so-subtle ways. To them, my most sincere thanks indeed. Finally, I wish to acknowledge my deep appreciation of Ms. Jan Wright, for her superb organization of the Symposium and for her skillful preparation of this book's manuscript.

Chapter One

The Realm of Childhood Sexual Abuse

An Introductory Overview

Salman Akhtar and Shawn Blue

In April 2018, the Pulitzer Prize–winning novelist, Junot Diaz, revealed that, as an eight-year-old child, he had been repeatedly raped. With words whose shimmering eloquence is only surpassed by the choking anguish they contain, Diaz described the devastating impact of this violation upon him.

> Not enough pages in the world to describe what it did to me. The whole planet could be my inkstand and it still wouldn't be enough. That shit cracked my planet in half, threw me completely out of orbit, into the lightless regions where life is not possible. I can say, truly, *que casi me destruyó*. Not only the rapes but all the sequelae: the agony, the bitterness, the self-recrimination, the *asco*, the desperate need to keep it hidden and silent. It fucked up my childhood. It fucked up my adolescence. It fucked up my whole life. More than being Dominican, more than being an immigrant, more than, even, being of African descent, my rape defined me. (2018, 12).

Not all victims of childhood sexual abuse are gifted with such expressiveness. They keep their suffering to themselves, become depressed, somatize, or develop myriad forms of post-traumatic symptoms and behaviors. It is such agony, often unspoken and yet inwardly devastating, that our contribution seeks to address. In tackling the dark realm of childhood sexual abuse, we will divide our comments into four sections, namely, (i) epidemiology, (ii) emotional sequelae (iii) psychoanalytic insights, and (iv) ameliorative strategies. This division is for didactic ease and does not wipe out the seepage of material from one to the other sections. We are keenly aware that phenomena of human lived experience, memory, subjectivity, and affect are hardly classifiable into neat and sacrosanct categories.

EPIDEMOLOGY

All sorts of questions emerge as one undertakes a thorough description of childhood sexual abuse. How prevalent is it? Are boys and girls victimized to the same extent? Who does the child report it to? What happens if there is no one trustworthy for the child to complain about what is being done to him or her? Are there family configurations, domestic environments, and parental personality characteristics that predispose a child to being sexually abused? And, of course, what impact does sexual abuse have upon a growing child's emotional life, sense of trust, and later capacity to form meaningful relationships, especially in the area of romantic love and sexuality? In order to deal with this plethora of questions, we divide our comments into three subsections: (i) incidence and prevalence, (ii) predisposing factors, and (iii) actual acts of abuse.

Incidence and Prevalence

Sexual abuse is one among the many forms of abuse that fall under a larger category of child maltreatment (Christoffel et al., 1992); other forms include physical abuse, neglect, and emotional maltreatment. Child maltreatment involves parental behaviors that cause substantial physical and emotional harm to their offspring. These behaviors include both acted upon and omitted behaviors as well as intentional and unintentional behaviors.

The U.S. Department of Health and Human Services (2017) has acknowledged that child abuse is a matter of significant concern to society and its health services. The entity that focuses on the neglect of children, the Children's Bureau, provides national statistics on the prevalence of child abuse based on information reported to agencies of child protective services (CPS) throughout the United States. The federal government has identified specific standards that guide each state's guidelines for cases of abuse to children. The criteria of abuse defined by the Child Abuse Prevention and Treatment Act (CAPTA) and the CAPTA Reauthorization Act of 2010 involves both actual acts or failures to act in behaviors that prove to be risky or pose harm to the child (i.e., emotional harm, sexual violation, physical injury, and/or death).

The collection and analysis of these reports is maintained through the National Child Abuse and Neglect Data System. It declares that of the 74 million children in the United States in 2015, 7.2 million were referred for child abuse investigation. Compared to 2011, this number represents a 15.5 percent increase. Reports to CPS are submitted by three different groups. The first group includes professionals who had interacted with children as a function of their occupation. The second group involves individuals who learn about abuse of children outside of a professional role; they include friends, relatives, and neighbors. The third group includes individuals who do not fall neatly into the previous two categories (i.e., religious leaders, community organizers, landlords, etc.). The highest number of reports received came from professionals (63.4%). Education and legal and law enforcement personnel submitted the majority of reports (18.4% and 18.2%, respectively). Social services (10.9%), medical personnel (9.1%), mental health personnel (5.8%), day care workers (.6%), and foster care providers (0.4%) also supplied reports. Nonprofessionals (18.2%) and unclassified sources (18.3%) reported in similar numbers with parents and other relatives (6.8%), friends and neighbors (4.2%), others (7.8%), and anonymous sources (7.4%) submitting the majority of these reports.

Situations of neglect are identified as the highest rate of child maltreatment (75.3%) as compared to physical abuse (17.2%) and sexual abuse (8.4%). Based on rates reported in 2014, 7.1 per thousand children were identified as experiencing neglect. "Polyvictimization" or a situation where children experience multiple forms of maltreatment was frequently reported. One common co-occurrence included the experience of neglect and sexual abuse (1.3%). In addition, sexual abuse cases made up 1.2% of fatalities (U.S. Department of Health and Human Services, 2017).

An important consideration in understanding these statistics is that cultural and subcultural variables play a role in prevalence rates of child sexual abuse. It appears that the experience of childhood sexual abuse is disclosed more often or even occurs with greater frequency more often in individual-oriented cultures (Mbagaya, 2010; Kenny and McEachern, 2000). This higher prevalence is attributed to such cultures' openness to discuss sexuality and sexual experiences, which involve a greater probability to disclose. However, Mbagaya (2010) suggested that differences might be the result of cultural and socioeconomic factors related to customs of socialization practices and a transition to more individualistic processes.

According to some recent data (U.S. Department of Health and Human Services, 2017), it appears that there is a decline in the occurrence of child sexual abuse with a decline in reported cases of sexual abuse (9% decline) and substantiated cases of sexual abuse (64% decline) from 1990–2014. However, it is unclear whether these numbers reflect the actual prevalence of child sexual abuse since they are dependent on the reporting of the child or another individual. Therefore, they do not encompass the number of cases of child sexual abuse that go undisclosed. In addition, these statistics do not illustrate other harmful behaviors (e.g., sexualized language, seductive conversations) can also affect children adversely and contribute to the premature sexualization of their weak egos.

Predisposing Factors

A review of the literature of child sexual abuse reveals a cumulative theory of risk factors, with the increased probability of experiencing maltreatment being correlated with the number of risk factors in a child's life (Begle, Dumas, and Hanson, 2010; MacKenzie, Kotch, and Lee, 2011). A history of previous sexual abuse (Bohm, Zollner, Fegert, and Liebhardt, 2014) also increases the chances of future sexual abuse. Furthermore, the existence of a disability also increases the risk of experiencing sexual abuse. Based on this cumulative theory of risk for abuse, the more disabilities (i.e., intellectual, behavioral, and communicative) an individual has, the greater is his or her risk for being sexually abused. When children who have disabilities experience sexual abuse, they also tend to experience more severe mental health issues (Mepham, 2010; Reiter, Bryan, and Shachar, 2007).

Another important factor involves the structure of the family. Family units that include stepparents or single parent households increase the risk of children experiencing sexual abuse, with foster homes or homes with a single parent and a live-in significant other having the highest risk (Sedlak et al., 2010). Family units that include drug and alcohol abuse also increase the risk of sexual abuse (Ammerman, Kolko, Kirisci, Blackson, and Dawes, 1999; Besinger, Garland, Litrownik, and Landsverk, 1999). Family units where parents have child abuse histories themselves increase the risk of children being the recipients of child abuse (DiLillo, Tremblay, and Peterson, 2000). In addition, family units that involve domestic violence and poor conflict resolution skills also increase the risk.

Age, race, and ethnicity and socioeconomic status are additional risk factors. Related to sexual abuse, the age before eight is significant (Snyder, 2000). When compared to white children, African American children are twice as likely to be the recipients of sexual abuse, with Hispanic children having a small increase of risk over white children (Sedlak et al., 2010). Social and economic risk factors include children in unemployed households, low socioeconomic households, and rural geographic areas (Sedlak et al., 2010). Children who are exposed to violence or crime or children who experience other types of crimes or abuse also serve as risk factors (Finkelhor, Ormrod, and Turner, 2010).

Reviewing studies of the type of children that perpetrators seek, it appears that they target children that are passive, quiet, or lonely and from single-parent homes (Elliott, Browne, and Kilcoyne, 1995). To obtain trust, perpetrators search for children with whom they spend a great deal of effort in building a trusting relationship before initiating abuse with the child (De Bellis, Spratt, and Hooper, 2011) and the child's family (Elliott et al., 1995). Male children have been found to be at risk for sexual abuse within the Catholic Church (Bohm et al., 2014) as a result of the large number of young males that interact with clergy (Terry and Freilich, 2012).

There are three major categories that describe sexual abuse perpetration: intrafamilial, extrafamilial, and institutional. In situations of intrafamilial abuse, the perpetrator is someone who lives with or has a biological relationship with the child. In cases of extrafamilial sexual abuse, there is no biological relationship or no previous relationship preceding the abusive relationship. A subcategory within extrafamilial sexual abuse perpetration is institutional abuse, which involves abuse that occurs at settings and organizations that provide services to youth (i.e., school, health care settings, after school programs, churches, daycare centers).

Sullivan et al. (2010) revealed that there are several risk factors that increase the chances of sexual perpetration and include impaired social and emotional functioning and regulation and problematic interests and attitudes regarding sex. When comparing the various types of sexual abuse perpetrators, institutional sexual abuse offenders tended to be diagnosed with pedophilia more often when compared to intrafamilial or extrafamilial offenders (Turner et al., 2016). Shakeshaft (2004) conducted a literature of institutional offenders in school settings and provided a profile of the type of offender within the educational setting. Within a primary school level, offenders typically are perceived to be "nice" and are well liked by those within their professional community. They also have usually received professional recognition. Within a secondary school level, offenders are typically not as distinguished as their peers. They tend to be focused on and have a high involvement in youth activities and are often perceived to be "creepy."

Important in considering prevention of child sexual abuse involves an understanding of the multiple risk factors involved in its occurrence and maintenance. Vulnerabilities in childhood increase one's risk in experiencing abuse. Personal vulnerabilities, such as having a disability, increases the chances one will experience abuse. Age, gender, ethnicity, and socioeconomic factors also increase a child's vulnerability in experiencing abuse. Familial vulnerabilities include single parent homes, exposure to a parent's significant other, parental abuse of drugs and alcohol, parental child abuse histories, and exposure to domestic violence. Additional risk factors involve the existence or lack of a biological relationship with the child or the setting that provides services to children. Grooming behaviors are utilized to increase the opportunity to abuse a child and grooming behaviors are targeted toward children and family members.

Actual Actions of Abuse

Sexual abuse of a child might occur suddenly and unexpectedly. This is often true when the abuser is a stranger and in the settings of kidnapping and sexual trafficking. More often, sexual abuse is insidious, sustained, and evolves out of the so-called "grooming" behavior. "Grooming" is a term to describe the behaviors used by perpetrators to prepare the child and his or her environment for the forthcoming violations. There are several components of a grooming process involving attempts to obtain access to the child. Offenders engage in behaviors to make the child succumb to their requests and demands. By requiring secrecy, the offender is able to maintain his or her abusive behaviors (Craven, Brown, and Gilchrist, 2006). In addition to grooming the child, the offender also participates in grooming of the adults around the child, with a purpose of creating a culture that will maintain the abuse. Grooming appears to become more coercive after other subtler behaviors are unsuccessful (Kaufman and Patterson, 2010; McAlinden, 2012). In addition, perpetrators are sensitive to the developmental level of their targets and will modify their behaviors to match the age and needs of the children they abuse (Kaufman et al., 1998). Turner and Briken (2015) found that sexual abuse perpetrators in institutional settings tend to differ in terms of intelligence by having higher IQs than intrafamilial and extrafamilial offenders.

The process of grooming behaviors is constituted by elements of relationship building, such as trust, validation, and nurturance (Kaufman and Patterson; 2010; Moulden, Firestone, Kingston, and Wexler, 2010). Children who are perceived to be vulnerable appear to be a risk factor for entering into a grooming relationship. In addition, other risk factors involve children who tend to be unassertive and are naïve regarding sexual behavior. Furthermore, risk variables related to the caretaking relationship include a low level of supervision in the home and the child's desire to have a caretaking relationship with an adult.

The nauseating impact of the foregoing passages is surpassed by a consideration of the kinds of physical violations perpetrated against children by their abusers. The range is broad and includes such acts as lasciviously looking at a child, rubbing against his or her body, masturbating in front of the child, having the child masturbate the perpetrator, fellatio, anal intercourse, vaginal intercourse, and insertion of foreign bodies into the children's perineal orifices. At times, this takes place in a pseudo-loving ambience. At other times, the child is forced to participate and is threatened with violence (to the child or to his or her loved ones) and stopped from revealing what went on. In either case, considerable "gaslighting" (see below) and break-down of the child's will and dignity occurs. This not only traumatizes the child in the current time but leaves a "long shadow" (Colarusso, 2010) of anguish on the psyche.

EMOTIONAL SEQUALE

Determining Variables

Sexual abuse of children results in a large variety of emotional and behavioral consequences. Among the factors responsible for the symptomatic variations are the following.

Relationship with the abuser: The effects of sexual abuse also vary in accordance with the relationship with the abuser, with the consequences being more grave and far-reaching in cases of incest (Margolis, 1977, 1991; Akhtar, 1991; Steele, 1991). This is because there is a greater sense of betrayal and a persistent need to depend upon one's family members.

Gender: Boys and girls respond rather differently to sexual violation. Perceptions of traditional male roles include expectations of strength, control and self-reliance. As a result, male children might experience conflict regarding their perception of strength and masculinity, which could lead to underreporting of abuse or underutilization of treatment. Additionally, men tend to not identify some types of sexual behaviors as abuse or will dismiss or deny abuse. Gender stereotypes tend to be especially high in youth sports and as a result, male children tend to underreport abusive acts. Male children can experience emotional sequelae including depression, anxiety, guilt, shame, lowered self-esteem, disordered eating, personality disorders (antisocial personality disorder and borderline personality disorder) and post-traumatic stress disorder. Similar to women who have experienced sexual abuse, men also have difficulty with intimacy in interpersonal relationships (Herman, 1992). However, while women tend to develop inhibitions in the realm of sexuality, men often identify with the aggressor and become sexually driven and promiscuous.

Child's age: The consequences of sexual abuse also vary, depending on the child's age and his or her epigenetically unfolding fantasy life. The extent to which the child has acquired verbal fluency also matters. Early and preverbal sexual abuse may get encoded as "somatic memories" (Kramer, 1990), or as an "unrememberable and unforgettable" trauma (Frank, 1969). Moreover, if the child has reached the Oedipal page then the vulnerability for self-blame increases since a core of primary intentionality is also existent in the child. Consequences of sexual abuse also depend upon whether the capacity for orgasm is present; this may be true of adolescents but is absent in younger children. In the latter, the wish for tension "discharge is expressed through the child's fainting or sometimes by a loss of sphincter control" (Shengold, 1989, p. 61).

Signs and Symptoms

Regardless of these variables, the fact remains that some symptoms are immediately discernable: fear, withdrawal, refusal to go to this or that home and/or to be left alone with this or that relative or stranger, excessive anxiety upon separating from reliable caretakers, nightmares, and many other types of avoidant and phobic behaviors. Other manifestations emerge over time and range broadly over ego functions, affects, fantasy life, metabolism of aggression, and, above all, later evolving capacities for relationships in the romantic and sexual sphere of life.

Early on, children who experience sexual abuse develop hypervigilance and hyperarousal (Herman, 1992). They gain skill in deciphering others' inner emotional states and subtle changes in nonverbal language and this is often executed in an automatic and unconscious manner. The child learns two methods of dealing with their abuser: an approach of avoidance or making amends. Children might attempt to run away, hide, or detract attention away from themselves. Hiding can be in the form of physical hiding and/or a hiding of one's emotional state. However, if avoidance does not work, children will shift to attempts at obedience. This cycle results in a validation of a perception of helplessness and also increases the child's efforts to maintain loyalty in a desire to be seen as "good." Finally, the abused child experiences a lack of protection. Children perceive parental figures as not caring and as committing a betrayal. Therefore, the child experiences a sense of abandonment.

In most circumstances, children are reinforced to maintain silence in order to continue the culture of abuse. Abused children find themselves in a sense of conflict. They must create future relationships based off a model of caretakers who are dangerous, negligent, untrustworthy, and unsafe. Basing future relationships after the model of early abusive ones leads children to enact the psychological defenses of denial, minimalization, rationalization, bargaining, displacement, suppression or dissociation. Abused children often develop idealized perceptions of others, which often results in conflict due to the ultimate use of splitting and reduction of one's ability to self-regulate.

Sexually abused children also experience an impaired relationship with their bodies (Herman, 1992). Based on a history of their bodies being controlled and manipulated by others, children must reestablish a sense of ownership, safety and trust with their bodies. Most importantly, abused children must create a sense of intimacy that does not involve abuse, manipulation or coercion. Even when abused children obtain rationalization of their abuse, they unfortunately continue to experience the residue of abuse within their bodies. Finally, abused children also experience a disruption in other biological regulation systems, including sleeping, feeding and elimination.

Another consequence of childhood sexual abuse is the emergence of a "double self" (Herman, 1992). With an immature developmental skill in rationalization, abused children engage in justification by accepting that their "badness" has caused the abuse. This justification process and sense of self-blame provides the child with meaning and a sense of power. It allows the child to develop goal-directed behavior and leads to beliefs that if they try hard enough, they can end the abuse and can even lead to perfectionistic ideals. Developmentally, this is relevant and incorporates the child's egocentrism, with the self being identified as the center of everything. It is also a consequence of an individual experiencing a traumatic event, in that one attempts to find meaning by looking to self and inner faults. In an abusive environment, this approach is met with continued reinforcement. In addition, abused children adopt responsibility for their abuser's behaviors and transgressions. By adopting an inner "bad" self, the child integrates the abuser and is able to maintain attachments with their abusing caregivers. Finally, the combination of the inner self as "bad" in addition to the integrated abuser creates the foundation of the child's personality. This double-self also involves the conflict with the inner "bad" self and the outward presentation of a "perfect" self, which reflects the abused child's inner feelings of fragmentation. However, children remain in fear that if others were to honestly "know" them, they would be rejected.

Other responses to sexual abuse include rage, deficient social skills, difficulty with conflict resolution and defensiveness. Abused children rely on external sources for regulation and comfort and as a result seek dependence on others. Herman (1992) described an emotional state of an abused child involving grief, anxiety, depression, panic, fury, and despair. In order to manage this emotional state, the abused child resorts to self-injury accompanied with an experience of dissociation and depersonalization. Other methods of regulation include purging, compulsive sexual acts or risky behaviors, and drug use. These methods are utilized in a desire to obtain well-being. Indeed, a combination of the use of dissociation, the creation of the fragmented personality and methods of regulation allow survival in the abusive culture (Kluft, 1990; Herman, 1992; Brenner, 1996).

Situations where abused children are forced into abusing others or recruiting others to be abused can elicit strong feelings of guilt and self-loathing. In an attempt to bargain as a way to save others, abused children will sacrifice themselves, which only leads to increased violence and abuse. Terr (1990) described how an abused child will play out their rage in three different ways: the first way involves an identification with the abuser and includes perpetrating abuse onto others; the second way includes a passive rage and acting out of a behavior utilized within their own history of experiencing abuse; the third and final way is to function in an appropriate way but when met with frustration or disappointment, these individuals will resort to rage filled behaviors.

Generally speaking, adults with abuse histories often have severe difficulties in setting healthy boundaries with others. This opens these individuals up to opportunities of ending up in future abusive or manipulative relationships. Although there is a small percentage of individuals with abuse histories who become perpetrators themselves, many individuals engage in aggressive behaviors toward themselves (i.e., self-injury and suicide) or find themselves in relationships with abusive others. In order to avoid having their own children experience abuse, some individuals with abuse histories put forth great efforts to provide protective caretaking for offspring (Herman, 1992).

The emotional responses and utilization of psychological defenses perfected as a child begin to break down as one becomes older. The ability to maintain healthy relationships and appropriate and adequate self-regulation and self-soothing become extremely difficult with the deficient skills mastered in childhood. Major life events serve as stressors that exacerbate what are already inadequate coping skills. What often occurs is psychological and personality disorders that make emotional and interpersonal functioning challenging. To survive a past of sexual child abuse, some individuals engage in a protective behavior, involving repression or denial of the details. Dissociative or numbing behaviors can also be employed to avoid or cope with the various psychological responses of the abuse.

PSYCHOANALYTIC INSIGHTS

Psychoanalytic literature on sexual abuse of children is voluminous. The electronic compendium of such writings over the last century (PEP web) includes nearly 200 entries and a considerable number of monographs devoted to this topic exist in addition (see details below). As a result, our survey of this corpus of knowledge will be selective. To assure that what we provide nonetheless reflects the evolving trends, we have divided our discussion into three subsections: (i) Freud's views, (ii) the views of his early followers, and (iii) the contributions of contemporary psychoanalysts.

Freud's Views

Early on in his career, Freud (1893, 1895, 1896) proposed that the symptoms of hysteria (a term applied during his days to a diverse group of conversion and dissociation based symptoms) and obsessional neurosis were caused by sexual "seduction" by adults during the patients' childhood. This came to be known later as his "seduction hypothesis." The "seduction" involved in such scenarios ranged from verbal and visual overstimulation to actual sexual abuse. The perpetrators were mostly parents but sometimes older siblings, other relatives, and domestic caretakers as well.

Freud suggested that the sexual trauma underlying adult neurotic symptomatology occurred in two stages. The first stage, where the actual event(s) took place, caused unease and fear but no sexual excitement in the child as the somatic requisites for such excitement were generally ill-developed then. This trauma was not repressed and remained in awareness, even though it did not consistently preoccupy the child's mind. The second stage consisted of an event that was not necessarily sexual in nature but revived the memory of the first event. This revival, owing to the doubling of affect (past and present), became disturbing and therefore underwent repression. Neurotic symptoms evolved later on from this very repression. In hysteria, it was the displaced enactment (via dissociation) or symbolic somatization (via conversion) that gave rise to symptoms. In either case, the revivification of childhood sexual trauma was the source of the hysteric's distress. In Freud's own words: "Hysterics suffer mainly from reminiscences" (1893, p 7). In obsessional neurosis, the additional feature of regression (and the associated omnipotence of thought) played a decisive role along with the defenses of reaction formation and undoing.

Tracing the evolution of these ideas in Freud's subsequent writings reveals that he began to doubt the veracity of his patients' reports of childhood sexual seduction quite early on. In a September 9, 1897 letter to his friend, Wilhelm Fliess, he stated, "I will confide in you at once the great secret that has been dawning upon me in the last few months. I no longer believe in my *neurotica*" (Freud, 1897, p. 223, italics in the original). This dropping of "seduction hypothesis" led Freud to a greater interest in intrapsychic origins of infantile sexuality. In a statement that heralded a monumental shift in psychoanalytic theorizing, Freud (1914) declared that,

> If hysterical subjects trace back their symptoms to traumas that are fictitious, then the new fact which emerges is precisely that they create such scenes in *phantasy*, and this psychical reality requires to be taken into account alongside practical reality. This reflection was soon followed by the discovery that these phantasies were intended to cover up the auto-erotic activity of the first years of childhood, and to embellish it and raise it to a higher plane. And now, from behind these fantasies, the whole range of a child's sexual life came to light (1914, pp. 17–18, italics in the original).

From there, the psychoanalytic view that hysteria and obsession were caused by childhood sexual trauma changed into the perspective that gave premium to infantile sexuality, fantasy, Oedipus complex, and so on. This decisive shift has led many subsequent investigators to assert that Freud totally abandoned the idea that children were often sexually abused by adults and that this resulted in their developing psychiatric symptoms later on. Three kinds of critiques are directed against Freud in this context: (i) the first is based upon the cynical assertion (Masson, 1984) that Freud denounced his "seduction hypothesis" out of the fear of retaliation by the Viennese bourgeois society, (ii) the second and more scholarly viewpoint (Ahbel-Rappe, 2006) is one which discerns that Freud, in his later work, showed a tendency toward reducing paternal incest to fantasy, nullifying the distinction between real and imagined seduction, and even in the face of acknowledging real incest, placing a greater emphasis on the contributions of infantile sexuality, and (iii) the third and psychohistorical proposal (P. Rudnytsky, personal communication, June 10, 2018). that Freud moved away from his "seduction hypothesis" to avoid the full impact of discovering that he might have been thus "seduced" by his childhood nurse maid and himself might have seduced his younger siblings.

A conciliatory note is struck by Laplanche and Pontalis (1973) in their highly respected and heavily footnoted study of Freud's theory. They note that, until the end of his life, Freud (1938) continued to regard childhood sexual abuse as one among the many determinants of adult psychopathology. Moreover, he refined his notion in this regard, adding (1916) that (i) it was sexual abuse by an older sibling in later childhood that was often retrospectively attributed to earlier periods and to parents, and (ii) that the infantile pleasures of being physically ministered by the mother could serve as a "ground of reality" (1933, p. 120) on which later fantasies of seduction can be built.

The Views of Freud's Early Followers

Even with Freud's move toward a greater emphasis on psychic reality and infantile sexuality, the theme of childhood sexual abuse continued to occupy the attention of his pupils and early followers. Two outstanding contributions among this body of work are those by Abraham (1907) and Ferenczi (1933). We have selected these two essays since they advocate contradictory viewpoints and highlight the post-Freudian evolution of psychoanalytic theory as it pertains to childhood sexual abuse.

Abraham's (1907) paper reflects a loyal attempt to reconcile Freud's "seduction hypothesis" and his later emphasis on the autonomous role of infantile sexuality. Abraham did not deny that children were sexually abused. However, he distinguished between those children who were unexpectedly victimized and those who were compliant, active participants, and even the provocateurs of their own exploitation. However, by devoting most of his paper to the latter group, Abraham ended up declaring that a child's being sexually abused to be "a masochistic expression of the sexual impulse [and] therefore representing one form of infantile sexual activity" (p. 54). The child's immediately telling or not telling an adult (e.g., the mother) about what has been done to him also attracted Abraham's attention. He attributed the child's not telling to his or her unconscious guilt at having sought the sexual seduction in the first place. This 1907 paper, while containing some interesting passages on the later accident-proneness of those who have been sexually abused as children, and providing a generous dollop of clinical vignettes, was marred by its "blaming the victim" mentality and a more than faint breath of misogyny that, unfortunately, permeated many psychoanalytic writings of its time.

In contrast, Ferenczi's (1933) paper, "Confusion of tongues between adults and the child," makes the emotionally powerful and clinically sound point that a love-deprived child seeks solace from the adult who, for the aims of his own sensual greed, "mistakes" this gesture for an erotic appeal and consequently sexually abuses the child. The child's affectionate "language of tenderness" is translated by the sensuality of the adult into the "language of passion"; this is the malevolent "confusion of tongues" that Ferenczi delineated in this paper. In his own words,

> A typical way in which incestuous seductions may occur is this: an adult and a child love each other, the child nursing the playful fantasy of taking the role of mother to the adult. This play may assume erotic forms but remains, nevertheless, on the level of tenderness. It is not so, however, with pathological adults, especially if they have been disturbed in their balance and self-control by some misfortune or by the use on intoxicating drugs. They mistake the child's play for the desire of a sexually mature person or even allow themselves—irrespective of any consequences—to be carried away (p. 161).

Unlike Abraham who regarded the child's submission to the adult's erotic advances as a manifestation of the child's own sexual desire, Ferenczi attributed such surrender to the child's psychic weakness and a mesmerized breakdown of self-boundaries in the face of enormous anxiety.

> These children feel physically and morally helpless; their personalities are not sufficiently consolidated in order to be able to protest, even if only in thought, for the overpowering force and authority of the adult makes them dumb and can rob them of their senses. *The same anxiety, however if it reaches a certain maximum, compels them to submit like automata to the will of the aggressor, to divine each one of his desires and to gratify them; completely oblivious of themselves, they identify themselves with the aggressor.* (p. 162, italics in the original)

Ferenczi also described what happens after the act of sexual abuse. The child feels confused and "his confidence in the testimony of his own senses is broken" (p. 162). Further complication is added by the fact that the abusive adult splits off his guilt at committing such violations and deposits into his child victim. Consequently, the child who is sexually abused feels guilty about what has just happened, despite the fact that the responsibility of it lay with the adult perpetrator. Ferenczi goes on to say the child is even more hurt if his or her mother is "not intimate enough for the child to find help there" (p. 163). The child feels guilty but knows that he is innocent but does not find a second adult to reinforce the latter conviction. Besides the guilty-innocent split that such a child develops, another split pertains to a "traumatic progression" (p. 165) into stoicism and precocious maturity on the one hand and a continued fixation upon the traumatic betrayal on the other hand. Ferenczi also observed that the child, incapable of climax as he or she is, merely feels a "sense of saturation" (p. 167) and not a release of tension by orgasm. This leaves the child psychosomatically suffused with sustained, if preconscious and vague, excitement. The passionate "love" and severe punishment by adults (if the child complains or threatens to complain during the act of sexual abuse) compounds the "terrorism of suffering" (p. 166).

The Contributions of Contemporary Psychoanalysts

Before tackling the important contemporary contributors to this realm, it must be underscored that Ferenczi's 1933 paper itself remains quite "contemporary"; its theoretical and clinical significance has hardly diminished with the passage of time. That being said, we turn our attention to contemporary psychoanalytic literature. The first thing we note is that of the 172 entries on "childhood sexual abuse" and "incest," over the past 100 years, 97 have been published in the decade of the 1990s. This contributes 56 percent of all literature on this subject. Why this particular decade should contain the majority of literature on sexual abuse of children is unclear. And, as if the PEP web derived "evidence" were not enough? We note that no less than five monographs on incest-related pathology (Ganzarian and Buchele, 1989; Kluft, 1990; Levine, 1990; Kramer and Akhtar, 1991; Herman, 1992) also made their appearances during this very period. Why this sudden burst of clinical reporting of childhood sexual abuse? Could it be that the psychoanalytic profession needed a long period of mourning after Freud's death in 1939 to "overcome" his Oedipal emphasis and begin paying attention to actual traumas of childhood? Could it be a reflection of the fact that after an intoxicated absorption in matters intrapsychic, psychoanalysis had woken up to what goes on in actual reality and how it affects human beings? Could the gradually evolving shift of attention in this direction and the resulting "anthropological psychoanalysis" (Akhtar, 2013) be responsible for this enthusiasm? Could the emergence of two-person relational models of theory and the associated rediscovery of Ferenczi and Sullivan have contributed to this rejuvenation of interest in early sexual trauma? Such questions might be unanswerable but the 1990s plethora of psychoanalytic contributions to the problem of childhood sexual abuse remains undeniable.

Clearly, it is not possible to satisfactorily cover such voluminous literature here and, as a result, we have opted to offer an alphabetized and annotated list of fresh concepts regarding patients with sexual abuse or incest in their backgrounds.

- *Attachment to the perpetrator* (Brenner, 2014) is a term used to explain the puzzling finding that the sexual abuse of a child often lasts long past the development in him or her of the capacity to say "no" and to fight off an assault against one's will. "Attachment to the perpetrator" is what prolongs the abuse and such adhesive bond evolves in part due to its beginning to gratify unconscious Oedipal impulses and the masochistic need for punishment arising from them.
- *Autohypnotic vigilance* (Shengold, 1989) refers to the hypercathexis of certain perceptual functions existing side by side with defensive obliviousness of other environmental cues; a person using this mechanism can simultaneously be an unbelievably trustworthy witness to what is going on and a completely unreliable observer.
- *Behavioral reenactments* (Terr, 1991) refer to physical actions and responses that repeat the original sets of thoughts or feelings (even if these were not registered as such then) at the time of sexual trauma.
- *Catastrophic aloneness* (Grand, 2002) denotes the sense of isolation that is beyond the limits of human tolerance. Originally described in the context of the humiliation, abuse, and violence that typifies the childhoods of serial killers, "catastrophic aloneness" is a concept equally applicable to a sexual abused child's subjective experience.
- *Dissociative adhesive state* (Grand, 1997) refers to the conviction of certain schizoid perpetrators of sexual abuse of their acts as "not actually *real*, not really *sex*, not really *me*" (p. 465, italics in the original). Such conviction arises from the fact that the incestuous acts involved take place within a prelinguistic modality and are not encoded in discursive, autobiographic memory.
- *Double denunciation* (Bigras, 1990) refers to the two-step process by which the analyst (i) explicitly validates the sexually abusive act to have been a violation and a crime, and (ii) acknowledges that certain features of the analytic situation (e.g., analyst's silence) can replicate the unhelpful and betraying aspect of the patient's early family situation.
- *False memories* (Loftus, 1993) refer to the skeptical view that, "recovered memories" (see below) of early childhood sexual abuse actually reflect a concordance between the analyst and patient and are based more upon suggestion than upon historical truth. (For a thorough review of this controversy, see Brenneis, 1994; Davies, 1996.)
- *Gaslighting* (Barton and Whitehead, 1969) refers to the perpetrator's effort to make the victim question the veracity of his own perception. Though not named as such, this notion was implicit in Ferenczi's (1933)

ideas about the impact of sexual abuse upon children and has been rejuvenated in Shengold's (1989) writing on "soul murder."

- *Mystification* (Apprey, 1991) refers to the process by which the psychic void caused by a secret sexual trauma is filled by a created reality. What is objective is thus subjectivized and "presented as bifurcated but continuous: inside and outside, present and absent, part and whole, high and deep" (p. 121). This concept has close links, as its proponent acknowledges, to Freud's (1900) "deferred action" and to certain ideas of Green (1973) and Khan, (1983).
- *Object-coercive doubting* (Kramer, 1983) denotes a clinical phenomenon resulting from sexual overstimulation of children by their mothers. It is characterized by the child's engaging the mother in endless arguments in which she is coerced into taking the opposite side of what the child feels is true at a given moment. Such coercion "often ends in orgasm-like fury for both, thus reenacting the sexual play between them" (p. 345). "Object coercive doubting" is distinct from obsessional doubting, which is derived from conflicting feelings within a tormented self; the former is experienced as emanating from the mother (or a maternal substitute) since the sexual stimulation in question has often occurred before the formation of adequate self and object boundaries.
- *Recovered memory phenomenon* (Loftus, 1993) refers to the fact that some patients recall for the first time during their analyses that they had been sexually abused as children. These patients had never known as adults, before their analytic treatment, that such an event had occurred. A proposal of this sort revivifies the ongoing debate between the importance of historical versus psychic reality (see the Freud-Ferenczi material above and also Spence, 1982; Brenneis, 1994).
- *Satanic ritual abuse* (Smith and Pazder, 1980) denotes the occurrence of sexual violation of minors under the perverse rationalizations provided by cults, pseudo-religious doctrines, and seemingly well-intentioned disciplinary activities. Such abuse was allegedly conducted by suburbanite white and economically affluent, if not wealthy, groups under conditions of great secrecy, and was accompanied by kidnapping, torture, and occult ceremonial acts. The sudden emergence of reports about this phenomenon during the 1980s stirred up a moral panic in the country. However, the proposal remained controversial, the testimonials of "victims" suspect, and its allegedly high prevalence dubious. By 1990s, skepticism about it grew in leaps and bounds (Putnam, 1991) and currently it is considered rare, though not entirely nonexistent.
- *Sitting duck syndrome* (Kluft, 1990) is the term for the monumentally increased vulnerability of those who have suffered early incestuous abuse to be sexually exploited by their therapists. The ego-weakness, the shame "deposited" by the perpetrators (Ferenczi, 1933), and the guilt incurred via

the child's own "moral defense" (Fairbairn, 1940) render such individuals weak and unable to resist their therapists" advances.

- *Somatic memories* (Kramer, 1991; Terr, 1991; Van der Kolk, 2014) designate the body's "recall" of circumstances associated with early sexual abuse. Often tactile, postural, or olfactory cues from the current environment mobilize sudden, dramatic, and convincing recollection of traumatic memories from the past. Whether somatic interactions can be intentionally employed during therapy in order to arouse such memories (with the aim of resolving them) remains an open question and a whole host of such techniques have evolved over the last few decades. (For a detailed bibliography on this, see Sletvold, 2014.)

Two caveats must be entered at this point. One, that the list above is incomplete; the psychoanalytic literature on sexual abuse of children is vast and we make no claim to be exhaustive in our coverage of it. Two, besides the concepts listed above, there are those which have appeared in completely different contexts but are also applicable to the realm of childhood sexual abuse. A prime example is the notion of a "joint acceptance of reality of the Holocaust" (Auerhahn and Laub, 1987), which declares that, in the treatment of Holocaust survivors and of their descendants, it is imperative that the analyst explicitly acknowledge that he knows and accepts that this great tragedy did take place. A similar need for validation applies to cases childhood sexual abuse. Other such concepts of extrapolated usefulness include "identification with aggressor" (A. Freud, 1946), "moral defense" (Fairbairn, 1940), "vertical splitting" (Kohut, 1977), and so on. And, finally, the meticulous refinements of the early concept of dissociation in the work of Brenner (1994, 1996, 2001) are also of great pertinence to the understanding and treatment of sexually abused patients.

AMELIORATIVE MEASURES

The wide-ranging discourse on the nature of childhood sexual abuse provided above has amply demonstrated the multilayered variables associated with the vulnerability, the occurrence, and the consequences of such violations. A corollary to this complexity is that ameliorative interventions in this realm have to be multipronged and often interdisciplinary. Keeping this in mind, we now offer some comments upon (i) individual psychotherapy and psychoanalysis, (ii) family-oriented interventions, and (iii) societal and legal measures, pertinent to this realm.

Individual Psychotherapy and Psychoanalysis

Based upon our own clinical experience and upon the various proposals made in the psychoanalytic literature, we believe that certain considerations must be kept in mind while treating patients with a childhood history of sexual abuse. We must emphasize though that we are not recommending specific strategies; what we are outlining in the passages below must be regarded as a background of attention that holds but does impart specific content to the therapeutic frame.

First: Many patients with a history of childhood sexual abuse are afraid of entering treatment with a therapist of the gender similar to that of the perpetrator. While gentle exploration of it during the initial consultation is certainly not out of place, generally speaking, the patient's wish for a therapist of this or that gender should be granted. This is especially important for adolescents (who are already undergoing phase-specific turmoil and are thus greatly prone to acting out) and for indigent patients (who come seeking help in psychotherapy clinics and have less say in to whom they are assigned for their care). Their asking for a particular gender therapist needs to be seen as self-protective and development-seeking, not as resistance. Abram's (1978) concept of "developmental interactions" and Pine's (1987) concept of "development work" should serve as guiding principles in dealing with clinical moments of this sort.

Second: It is important to remember that due to the tenacity of defenses, compulsion to repeat, and the complex transference-countertransference issues such patients bring forth, psychoanalysis or psychoanalytic psychotherapy is the preferred treatment for them. Clearly, this is only feasible when the personality damage is not too severe, psychological-mindedness exists, and reality factors (e.g., time, money, availability of analytic therapists) are favorable. However, even when psychoanalysis or two-three times per week psychoanalytic psychotherapy is not feasible, the theoretical and practical knowledge derived from psychoanalysis can be invaluable in helping such patients (Kramer, 1991).

Third: It should be kept in mind that not only patients with childhood sexual abuse and even incest mention such traumatic events at the very beginning of their treatment. Moreover, these unfortunate occurrences are found in all socioeconomic, ethnic, racial, and religious groups. The psychotherapist must therefore keep his or her mind open to the possibility that a most "unlikely" patient's past may turn out to include a history of childhood sexual abuse or incestuous trauma.

Fourth: Since many patients with a background of childhood sexual abuse tend to recreate sexually dangerous situations (in the hope of mastering them), the therapist has to be especially vigilant for the signs of such "inverted" seduction.

Clinical Vignette: 1

> Layla Aafandi, a thirty year-old pharmacist of Iranian origin, came to her first interview in a revealing dress. The neckline of her blouse swooped down to reveal a major portion of her breasts, and her skirt was up to her mid-thigh region. Even more strikingly, she "sat" on the chair in a nearly lying down posture. Her legs were extended and one of her feet came very close to mine. I was made uncomfortable by this and immediately suspected that she had been sexually abused as a child. However, I did not pull my foot back quickly. I waited and went on to hear her story and collect pertinent information. Soon, the history of childhood sexual abuse (by her father) came out. At this point, I gently withdrew my foot and pointed out that her manner of sitting, which created the possibility of physical contact between us, might have been related to what had happened in her past. Perhaps she was unwittingly inducing the discomfort of unwelcome proximity in me so that I could emotionally know what she had felt as a child. Besides, it seemed that she was also testing the safety of being with me. These remarks led to her sitting more erect, crying, and gradually revealing a history of much sexual exploitation, including two rapes, during adult life.

The risk of "boundary violations" (Gabbard and Lester, 1995) is forever present under such circumstances and need to be worked through.

Fifth: A corollary to the foregoing material is constituted by countertransference experiences that are quite private, incomprehensible, and not readily traceable to something the patient has said or done. The following case illustrates this well.

Clinical Vignette: 2

> During the first year or so of Rene Branch's treatment, I would often have a visual image in which a little baby was pierced by a long spear. Bleeding and still attached to the end of the spear, the baby spun helplessly. I felt no strong emotions with this image, just a vague puzzlement and curiosity. Only after some self-reflection was I able to sense in me the presence of much anxiety about this image. Still later, I could feel (alternately) both the tragic pleading, as it were, of the infant and the triumphant sadism of whoever held the spear (not a part of the image). It was, however, a long time afterward that the patient began talking of intense, ruthless, guilt-ridden impulses of stimulating children's genitalia until they were bleeding and squirming with painful pleasure. And it was still later that we were able to reconstruct that the patient's own genitals had been traumatically overstimulated by her mother, who had long nails painted red (the bloody spear!).

Sixth: Besides such countertransference signals, the emotional state of the therapist during clinical work with sexually abused individuals can provide or obfuscate other significant pieces of information. Kramer (1991) has noted that many therapists find it abhorrent to consider that mothers can be the perpetrators of a child's sexual abuse and change the topic when such material begins to surface. Other analysts (Margolis, 1991; Apprey, 1991; Simon and Bullock, 1994) have commented upon the difficulty therapists experience in listening to a patient's recollections of incest. The therapist working with such patients has to have the capacity to bear much sadness, horror, shame (in identification with the patient), and much contempt and revenge fantasies (toward the perpetrator). Moreover, the analyst has to be aware that such patients are extremely sensitive to betrayal. He or she must maintain reliability and consistency of the therapeutic frame. Raphling (1994) warns that "if the analyst does not keep abreast of how is actual behavior is affecting the abused patient, acting out may ensue and the working relationship will deteriorate" (pp. 55–56).

Seventh: Reconstruction of childhood sexual abuse, especially if it occurred very early on, is a slow, painstaking, and often incomplete process (see the clinical vignette #2). An additional fact that needs to be kept in mind here is that defenses erected against the contemporaneous recognition and the subsequent recall of childhood sexual abuse can themselves result in psychopathology, which warrants attention on its own accord.

Finally: All the care, caution, and tenderness implied in the forgoing suggestions must not be construed as a counsel against the "trio of guideposts" (Pine, 1997) constituted by anonymity, abstinence, and neutrality that characterize all analytically-oriented work. And, interpretive stance (vis-à-vis defensive distortions of memory, self-agency, and assignment of responsibility) must not be renounced. The following pithy statement by Gabbard (1997) serves as a highly useful reminder in this context.

> The pressure to act instead of think, to become entrenched in a persecutor/victim model of pathology that denies the autonomy and efficacy of the patient, and to become the real love object of the patient to heal wounds from the past all need to be noted, contextualized, and brought forth as part of the analytic discourse. A balance between the judicious use of affirmation and interpretation must be maintained so that both conflict and deficit are addressed in the course of treatment. The contemporary analyst, in other words, strives for a middle ground between Freud and Ferenczi. While the analyst must provide a good object experience and facilitate the analytic process, the object provided cannot be "too good." In fact, he or she must be a "bad enough object" (Rosen, 1993) so that the patient can re-experience and work through bad object experiences from the past (p. 21).

Family-Oriented Interventions

There have been several theories credited to explaining the intergenerational practice of child sexual abuse. Ney (1992) offered that maladaptive family behaviors have a role in the observation of child sexual abuse throughout generations. According to this theory, families engage in violence in order to obtain insight into maladaptive histories. If insight is not gained and the conflict remains unresolved, when individuals reach adulthood, they tend to utilize similar behaviors in another attempt to gain understanding. A triangle is formed within this theory that involves the perpetrator, victim, and observer, with interchanging roles and behaviors.

Interventions targeting the family in addressing issues of sexual abuse can be categorized into developmental models, parent-training programs, and family systems treatment (Wolfe, 1994). Developmental models focus on the interpersonal interactions within the family as well as an assessment of parenting skills. In addition, these models explore parental perceptions of children and parental ability to emotionally self-regulate during stressful parenting events. Most parent-training programs are based on a cognitive behavioral treatment approach and include education regarding behavioral interventions. The family systems approach focuses directly on aspects of the dynamic relationships within families.

Another treatment approach to family interventions includes home-based services and parent-enhancement programs. These services are concerned with the total needs of families. They also focus on social factors that affect families, including poverty, single parent homes, and conflict within the marital unit. The effectiveness of this type of service includes its integration of the multitude of stressors that affect families. This approach also allows for treatment that would not be afforded within traditional settings, such as in a private practice office, or in a community mental health center. Parent-enhancement programs are often utilized to improve the interactions between parents and children in families where sexual abuse has been identified, and can focus on such skills as appropriate discipline and emotion regulation. Family preservation programs have the goal of maintaining the family system and when appropriate avoid foster care. Other incentives of these programs include a wide range of therapeutic options and services (Crosson-Tower, 2002). The Patient Protection and Affordable Care Act created a program called the Maternal, Infant, and Early Childhood Home Visiting Program (MIECHV). Supported by the Health Resources and Services Administration (HRSA) and the Administration for Children and Families (ACF) this program provides home based visiting programs to enhance the health and functioning of children (U.S. Department of Health and Human Services, 2017).

One of the tasks of familial therapeutic interventions involves treating the dynamic relationship between the child who has experienced sexual abuse and the non-perpetrating parent (Levenson and Morin, 2001). The non-perpetrating parent can also benefit from individual therapy. The goals of individual therapy would involve addressing any emotional symptoms resulting from the child's sexual abuse, the impaired relationship with the abused child, and any potential intrapersonal issues, such as a personal history of sexual abuse, poor communication and boundary-setting skills, and a lack of an ability to establish structure or to take responsibility.

In a family systems approach to treatment, the family is viewed as interconnected (Zastrow and Kirst-Ashman, 2004). Within this approach, the experience of sexual abuse influences all members of the family. Several areas of family functioning are addressed in order to inform treatment and to offer relevant interventions and include an exploration of power structure, cohesion and autonomy, family roles, communication and problem-solving skills (Kilpatrick and Holland, 1999). A realistic acknowledgment of the occurrence of sexual abuse is sought within treatment. The perpetrating and non-perpetrating parental caretakers both take responsibility for the existence of the abuse and the lack of protection. The familial environment is also important when treating cases of sexual abuse. The environment includes extended family members, community members and friends, as well as religious institutions, medical and mental health services, and other groups and organizations.

Therapeutic interventions targeting families in situations of sexual abuse are one of many other services provided to strengthen the family. Other services include medical services that come into contact with the child or family members in conducting medical care. Protective services handle suspicions of child abuse and make determinations of whether a child is safe to stay in the home. Welfare services can provide economic aid in situations of financial need. Legal services offer assistance in situations of sexual abuse and make decisions related to the safety and treatment of the abused.

As a result of the fact that there are multiple risk factors related to the family that increase the chances of sexual abuse occurring, it is important to highlight these factors for the purpose of treatment. Socioeconomic status (SES) is a concern related to the occurrence of sexual abuse due to the higher risk of children being sexually abused from low SES households (Peter, 2009). It is suggested that this occurs due to lowered resources and the need for additional work in order to financially sustain the household. However, this provides a vulnerability that children will experience less supervision and monitoring and/or a need to be taken care of by others. The relationship with parents and parental mental health has also been associated with a risk factor of child sexual abuse. Having an uninvolved or absent father was associated with child sexual abuse in girls (Finkelhor and Baron, 1986) and boys, especially in the Catholic church (Fater and Mullaney, 2000; Isley et al., 2008). Being unemployed, having a disability, and having interpersonal conflict in the romantic relationships of mothers also served as a risk factor (Finkelhor and Baron, 1986).

Given the risk factors described above it is important for family therapeutic interventions to target these areas when considering treatment. Financial support would help families with low SES to obtain adequate resources to care for the child with not only necessities but also by decreasing the needs for childcare outside of the home. In addition, financial support would potentially lower stress associated with inadequate funds and would allow parents to be able to provide more attention to children and improve their interpersonal interactions.

Resources in the area of appropriate childcare would be helpful in providing assistance to one parent homes or two parent homes with lowered support systems. Appropriate childcare would also reduce the need for caretakers to be vulnerable in selecting child care providers or surrogate caretakers. Yet another intervention would include providing assistance for families with disabilities. Related to family strengthening, it would be important to offer skill building in the areas of boundary setting, conflict resolution, healthy expressions of loving behaviors, and affect regulation. Psychiatric treatment of any existing mental health issues would also be beneficial.

Conceptualizing one's community and society as a *family* and interventions to strengthen these relationships are important as well. Providing psychoeducation of healthy behaviors would be essential. Building better interactions and improving the understanding of gender roles also is needed. Encouraging more reporting of suspected abuse and serving as allies and protectors of children is essential. More education is a needed to be able to provide opportunities for children to feel comfortable disclosing their abuse and providing a protective environment when they disclose. Improving the foster care system and legal system would also help ensure better protection of children in cases of sexual abuse.

The importance of familial interventions in treating the occurrence of child sexual abuse is clear. It is important to address all family members within treatment whether the parent perpetrated the abuse or not. Skill building to strengthen the family in addition to therapeutic services to address the traumatic consequences of the abuse are essential to the healthy functioning of the family. Providing resources to address vulnerabilities of families, which might prevent their effective functioning, are also important. Finally, improving the supportive behaviors of the child's community and society as a whole are important in the eradication of child sexual abuse.

Social and Legal Measures

Children who have been sexually abused can resist disclosing their abuse for many reasons resulting from multiple emotions, such as fear or guilt. The probability of disclosing child sexual abuse increases when children experience that the individual is perceived to be non-judgmental and when they appear to already have knowledge of the abuse. Also, if children have been injured, provided with prevention literature or resources, or if they believe that the abuse is unbearable or are in fear of another child being abused, they are more likely to disclose their abuse.

Most referrals (or reports) to CPS agencies result in an investigation with the goal of establishing the occurrence or risk of maltreatment and to ascertain services. In situations where the risk has been identified to be low or moderate, alternative services are utilized. In cases of sexual abuse, several states do not allow alternative responses and require an investigation of the abuse. Once a report is submitted to a CPS agency, there is a twenty-four-hour to several-day time frame to obtain contact with the child of the suspected abuse (U.S. Department of Health and Human Services, 2017).

Investigations of child abuse are dependent on whether the perpetrator is related or not. Interfamilial investigations of child sexual abuse are handled by local child protection agencies, whereas local law enforcement agencies handle extrafamilial child sexual abuse. For interfamilial abuse, the first step in the legal process includes a report to CPS, which can be made from various sources (i.e., medical or mental health provider, teacher, neighbor, family member, etc.). Protective service officials investigate all reports to assess whether they are substantiated. If reports are substantiated child protective services provide referrals for treatment and oversee the monitoring of the child's safety (U.S. Department of Health and Human Services, 2017).

When the need for foster care is identified, the child who has experienced abuse is removed from the home and placed with a family that has been designated to foster and take care of the child. In certain cases, a child can be placed in temporary foster care, which provides time for the family members to improve the situations of the home and to increase safety within the home. When there appears to be little or no chance of improvement in the home, the child might be removed permanently and parental rights terminated. Although the positive benefit of foster care includes providing safety to a child who has been experiencing abuse, unfortunately, foster care environments also can potentially become new situations of abuse. The reality of new abuse occurring in foster care elicits conflict over the practice of removing abused children from the home. Also, the confounding discrimination of increased rates of removal of poor children complicates the legal process (Katz et al., 1986). To ensure safety, all children in a household might be removed if there is concern that danger remains of maltreatment in the home (U.S. Department of Health and Human Services, 2017). Alternatively, non-abused children can be removed voluntarily from the home by the parent and placed into foster care.

Some cases of sexual abuse end up being tried in legal proceedings (i.e., juvenile court, family court, criminal court). It is important to acknowledge the potential additional trauma of separation from the family unit, visitation, or custody cases. Criminal proceedings can mandate treatment for individuals who have been found guilty of sexually harming a child. There are many factors that complicate the legal proceedings of sexual abuse cases. In certain cases, there is a lack of evidence to substantiate the case. There is also the concern of the traumatic experience of the legal process on the child, including having to testify against his or her abuser. On the other hand, one of the larger concerns involve the lack of prosecution or inadequate treatment of abusers resulting in the continuation of abuse toward the child. Criminal and civil statutes of limitations for child sexual abuse cases have been extended in many states. The delayed discovery rule suspends the statutes of limitation in two situations: in the case of a repressed memory of abuse and a lack of awareness that prior abuse is causing current problems.

Evidence used in legal proceedings includes disclosures of sexual abuse by children. Roland Summit described a model called the "child sexual abuse accommodation syndrome" (CSAAS), which outlined how children who experience intrafamilial sexual abuse make disclosures of their abuse (Summit, 1983). His model included five factors that influence why children might avoid disclosing abuse and include (i) secrecy, (ii) helplessness, (iii) entrapment and accommodation, (iv) delayed, conflicted, and unconvincing disclosures, and (v) retraction of disclosure. Summit (1983) observed that when children do disclose their abuse, they often do so over time, with potential alterations between denying and recanting the abuse. The complication with disclosures of sexual child abuse involves the historical disbelief of children who easily disclose their abuse. Unfortunately, children were considered more credible if they engaged in denial, disclosure, recantation and re-disclosure of abuse (Summit, 1983). In addition, a child's disclosure does not always result in the cessation of the abuse (Palmer, Brown, Rae-Grant and Loughlin, 1999).

There are also concerns related to the testimony of children against their abuser(s). Due to the vulnerability of young children, they can have impressionable memories of the past. As a result, there is worry related to the potentiality of distorted or false memories (Lynn, Lock, Loftus, Krackow, and Lilienfeld, 2003; McNally, 2005) in children who experience child abuse and obtain therapeutic services. The legal prosecution system could have desires to delay the utilization of services until after proceedings are concluded in an attempt to avoid situations of distorted or false memories. The outcome of this approach involves abused children not receiving needed services to treat their abuse. Both the psychological and legal communities are invested in how therapeutic services influence the accuracy of memories (Ghetti et al., 2006; Nadel, Campbell, and Ryan, 2007). Despite many benefits of psychological services, there are several concerns that can produce potential errors in memory. In an attempt to address the trauma of abuse within psychotherapy, children often recount details of the abuse. Mental health providers or others (Bruck and Ceci, 1999; Principe and Schindewolf, 2012) close to the child could provide or reinforce inaccurate information and can alter the memories of children.

One recent longitudinal study explored the effect of psychological services obtained during or after legal proceedings and its influence on the accuracy of memory (Goodman, Goldfarb, Quas, and Lyon, 2017). Participating in psychological services resulted in a higher probability of the long-term accuracy of memory of abuse relevant details. It was also revealed that the utilization of psychological services did not increase the probability of memory errors. Authors theorized that therapeutic services provided enhanced understanding and cohesion and aided in memory accuracy. In addition, it was theorized that the reduction of trauma related symptoms also increased the accuracy of memory.

Several national violent and sexual events led to the institution of laws to protect individuals from violent crimes. One particular event involved the rape and murder of seven-year-old Megan Kanka by a convicted sex offender, Jesse Timmendequas, in 1994. In response, concerned individuals lobbied for laws that would help ensure protection from sexual offenders. Megan's Law became effective in 1996, which mandated community notification and registration of sexual offenders. Since then, states and the federal government have passed similar legislation. As a result of these laws, state authorities must notify communities that individuals with a sexual offense history are moving into the neighborhood. In addition, sex offenders must register their name and residence to local law enforcement agencies. The Federal Bureau of Investigation (FBI) upholds a nationwide registration system of sex offenders.

The Justice for Victims of Trafficking Act was signed into law by Barack Obama in 2015. The law requires states to provide a report of the numbers of children who are identified as being sex trafficking victims (U.S. Department of Health and Human Services, 2017).

It is important to acknowledge the significance of the legal process in cases of child sexual abuse. Foster care can provide opportunities to escape abusive environments but can exacerbate the trauma of sexual abuse if the foster home is another setting of abuse. Addressing the multiple traumas resulting from sexual abuse itself and separation from the family are important when children are removed from the home.

There are many concerns that exist during legal proceedings, related to the additional trauma to the child and insufficient treatment of perpetrators of abuse. There are many factors that support or prevent children from disclosing when they experience sexual abuse. Improving societal care of children's safety is important as well as the intersection of the legal system on obtaining disclosures during the legal process. More information related to sex trafficking is significant as well as the particular consequences of trafficking on child functioning.

CONCLUDING REMARKS

In this contribution, we have offered a wide-ranging survey of literature on childhood sexual abuse. We have divided our comments into four major sections of epidemiology, emotional sequelae, psychoanalytic insights, and ameliorative strategies. This approach has permitted us to cover epidemiologic data, demographic correlates, vulnerability factors, psychopathological symptoms, developmental vicissitudes, intrapsychic damage, psychotherapeutic strategies, family-based interventions, and societal and legal measures necessary to control or at least diminish the quantity of this major public health problem. Culled out of this extensive discussion are the following "take-home" points:

- Sexual abuse of children is widespread. Almost 8 percent of boys and 15 percent of girls may be sexually abused during their formative years.
- Being raised by a single parent, living in a foster home, having parents who abuse alcohol and drugs, being African American, having a disability, and coming from families rife with domestic violence increase the chances of a child being sexually abused.
- The emotional impact of childhood sexual abuse is multifaceted and lifelong. A great variety of psychosocially maladaptive behaviors and subjectivity distressing symptoms can be caused by such violations. These include mild-to-severe ego distortions, vulnerability to repeat the sexual trauma, mistrust, problematic love object choices, and disturbances of self-esteem.
- The psychopathology of the perpetrator has received less attention in the literature. However, it seems likely that individuals who sexually abuse children are themselves quite impaired. Lack of self-confidence, misplaced and eroticized idealization of one's affection toward children, superego defects, conscious or unconscious destructiveness toward a child who is deeply envied, and situational vulnerabilities (e.g., alcoholism, sexual and emotional deprivation) all combine to make the heinous betrayal of a child's trust possible.
- Of necessity, ameliorative strategies in this realm must be multipronged. They must address individual psychopathology resulting from having been abused. (The complexities of working with sexually abused patients have been highlighted above.) In addition, family-based interventions often need to be in place. Societal and legal measures are also necessary.

- The last-mentioned category must also address the nefarious realm of child pornography, sexual trafficking, and "sexual slavery." Interdisciplinary teams are required to evolve meaningful strategies to tackle this difficult and often crime-ridden terrain.

These elements of knowledge provide the conceptual screen upon which further nuanced material contained in this book is projected. Matters that the reader shall now encounter include clinical approaches to young children who have been sexually abused, the seduction of adolescent boys by their female teachers and its deleterious consequences, and, very importantly, the diabolical realm of sex-trafficking whereby innocent children and adolescents (mostly girls) are psychically entrapped, terrorized, and exploited for the aims of perverse adult sexuality. Following these chapters (and their respective discussions), a summarizing commentary by a distinguished colleague will bring this volume to a close while simultaneously opening up new vistas for clinical and sociopolitical thought and praxis.

Chapter Two

Clinical Interventions with Sexually Abused Children

Thomas F. Barrett

In her paper, "Children Who Were Raped," Anny Katan (1973) referred to Leonard Shengold's (1963) writings on children who had been sexually abused by a psychotic parent. She agreed with his observation that children who had been overwhelmed, overstimulated, or abused were compelled throughout their lives to create repetitions of what they had endured in an attempt, albeit a futile one, at ultimate integration and mastery. It was the opinion of both Katan (1973) and Shengold (1979), who later wrote extensively about "soul murder," a term allied with the developmental consequences of child sexual and emotional abuse, that it is only when efforts to repeat an abusive experience can emerge in analytic material and be recognized in the transference, that patients can begin to gain insight that can foster reconstruction, remembering and the ultimate working through that can lead to the relative mastery of early trauma. The six patients studied and reported upon by Katan were all women who in every case had repressed what had happened to them. For each, the feelings attached to the abusive event had been displaced onto other relationships, often onto their relationships with their fathers. In that context, there could occur a merging and blending of what had happened at the time of the abuse with other exciting and seductive experiences, as well as elaborations of fantasies that came from those experiences and from the patients' own instinctual impulses. It was only in analysis that the resulting entanglement could be sorted out and understood.

It is the compulsion to repeat that is often a factor in bringing sexually abused young persons to the attention of professionals. This is particularly true of teenagers. The transition into adolescence, with its intensification of feelings and impulses, compels the return of memories or conflicts previously repressed. In addition to the compulsion to repeat, turning passive into active and turning aggression against the self are defensive maneuvers that appear.

A VIGNETTE OF AN ADOLESCENT CASE

Amy, a girl in her early teens, was referred for evaluation after severely cutting her wrist. Ten stitches had been required to close the wound. Amy explained to me that on a day off from school, she had been home with friends, unsupervised, when she suddenly became overwhelmed with anger without knowing why. When a friend spilled some paint, making a mess, Amy had snapped at her. Almost immediately, she felt so guilty that she went to the bathroom, took a razor from the cabinet and with her friends watching and screaming in horror, she ran into the yard where she dramatically and impulsively slashed at her wrist.

Amy's clinical presentation was highlighted by her unusual hairstyle. Half of her hair was cut very short, almost shaved, while the other half remained long and fell across her face, covering one of her eyes. The hairstyle seemed to announce how she felt "torn down the middle," struggling with the "good" and "bad" parts of herself that she felt unable to integrate. When talking about the effects of her suicidal gesture on her friends, she excitedly described how "they really flipped out!"

Amy's parents had divorced when she was five. Her father had been an alcoholic. She claimed to have no memories of the time preceding or following the breakup except to recall how she'd been cared for by an elderly woman who lived in a neighboring apartment while her mother had worked part-time. Amy recalled peaceful times spent playing on the woman's piano; the telling of this memory seemed to ward off the more volatile memories from her own apartment. Gradually, she explained how, after the divorce, her mother had become involved with a boyfriend who had a thirteen-year-old son who'd become Amy's babysitter. Over the course of several months, he had molested her, requiring her to fondle his genitals. After she could finally tell her mother what was happening, the mother broke up with the boyfriend and ended all contacts. During the time of being molested, Amy had developed an "enlarged colon," likely a consequence of a withholding symptom. She had also suffered nightmares and sleepwalking episodes that led to her sleeping each night with her mother.

Amy described to me that as a young teenager her favorite activities included reading scary books and watching horror movies. She admitted to difficult peer relations, especially with boys, as she impulsively went from one boyfriend to another, unable to sustain a relationship. She was not sexually active but admitted to being flirtatious and provocative.

The evaluation noted a parallel between Amy's early childhood experiences that had left her vulnerable to abuse and the day off from school at home without her mother's supervision. Her excitement with friends had culminated in her self-hurtful gesture. The excitement and the mess of the spilled paint had threatened to remind her of the thirteen-year-old babysitter and the "mess" of his ejaculations. She had tried to defend against her feelings by turning passive into active, shocking her friends as they were made to watch her make a liquid come from her body in a way that caused them to "really flip out!" Perhaps the "bloody show" had also been a response to the recent onset of her menstruation, another event Amy was struggling to integrate.

This example serves as an illustration of how the effects of an abusive experience endure within a developing personality, resulting in long-term and potentially destructive consequences as such a young person attempts to integrate her adolescent development. By the time Amy was molested at six years of age, she had already achieved a relative degree of ego development. Though she became symptomatic with withholding issues, nightmares, and sleepwalking, she had been able to reveal the trauma to her mother who was able to protect her from further abuse. Subsequently, she was able to repress the experience so that she could continue functioning. With the predilection to regression that often accompanies the onset of adolescence however, Amy lacked sufficiently available drive fusion to prevent the impulsive and dramatic self-hurtful act that led to her evaluation and referral for treatment.

In her paper, Katan (1973) revealed that all her adult patients had been at least three-years-old before they were abused. She emphasized that the most debilitating consequence of childhood sexual abuse is the resulting disturbance in drive fusion. As occurred for this young adolescent girl, unfused aggression can be viciously turned against the self. Katan stressed that when such a young person is sexually abused, they lack adequate pathways for discharge. I suspect that many sexually abused patients seen in analysis as adults are ones who had already achieved relative ego development (i.e., including the attainment of episodic or "explicit" memory).

By contrast, many child analysts have had the experience of treating children who were sexually abused at an even younger age, (i.e., age two or earlier), before the relative attainment of "explicit" memory. For these children, preverbal, implicit memories of an unconscious, emotionally tinged nature carry the residue of early trauma with the result that they may have failed to maintain progressive development. Such young, abused, children typically present with profound and pervasive impairment in ego functioning. Without early treatment, as they advance through childhood and into adolescence they might be labeled as "borderline," "atypical," or even "psychotic"; they might be institutionalized, placed in residential treatment, or maintained in "special" school programs and be medicated with an array of psychopharmaceuticals that typically include powerful anti-psychotic medications.

Among the relatively small number of articles focusing on analytic work with children with severe and early disturbances, Erna Furman (1956) published important case material and also other articles on traumatized (1986) and "atypical" (1998) children. In those papers, Furman described the behaviors, symptoms, and defenses characteristic of children traumatized at an early age. She details how such children have failed to achieve dominance at any developmental phase with residual conflicts from all phases persisting and coexisting. Aggressive conflicts are characterized by primitivity, destructiveness, and poor drive fusion. There is minimal available neutral energy to promote and support ego development and functioning which tends to be broadly impaired, unevenly invested, and almost never autonomous, remaining vulnerable to regression. Some functions (e.g., perception, speech, etc.) become defensively hypercathected. Such children are easily overwhelmed or made anxious and cannot well verbalize or modulate expressions of affect. They show poor self- and object-differentiation and fragile boundaries between inside and outside, self and other, past and present, and real and not real. Defenses are immature and often ineffective. Synthesis and integration are especially difficult for these children.

Furman comments that such children are often eager to begin therapy; they seem to yearn for help. For some, overwhelmed or out-of-control behavior may serve as a defensive barrier that strives to preserve an underlying ego core. For many though, initial gains can be deceiving as apparent improvements are often followed by setbacks and much reworking is required to gradually strengthen their impaired and limited integrative capacities.

In recent years, with the maturation of the field of infant and early childhood mental health (IECMH), several authors, including Pynoos (1990, 1993), van der Kolk (1987, 1996, 2014), and Liberman and her colleagues (2008, 2011, 2015) have linked the experience of such early trauma with patterns of bodily expression of residual affects; profoundly disorganized attachment; and later characterization and diagnosis of post-traumatic stress disorder. As more children have been identified as being on the autistic spectrum and/or ADHD, Schore (2001) has noted that we are challenged to differentially diagnose children with early histories of abusive trauma, including sexual abuse.

Regarding intervening with such children, Liberman and Van Horn (2008) emphasize how essential it is to work with traumatized young children in a way that closely involves their parents or primary attachment figures. Like Katan (1961), who emphasized the value of verbalization of affect for young children, Liberman and Van Horn (2008) emphasize the importance of clinicians being able to speak with children (and parents) about abusive trauma, including when, during treatment, the residue of implicit/feeling memories becomes available for articulation and acknowledgment.[1]

About treatment, Furman (1998) stresses that careful attention must be given to technique. Since traumatized young children are so vulnerable to feeling overwhelmed, it is important to provide a containing experience, carefully preparing them for interpretive comments. It can even be helpful to move slowly or minimally and to speak with a soft, gentle voice. Care must be given to prepare well in advance for vacations or separations from the therapy routine.

CLINICAL WORK WITH PRESCHOOL-AGE CHILDREN

The Case of Ben

Ben was three when he and his parents were referred to me by his therapeutic preschool. In the nursery setting, he had seemed unhappy, distant, and preoccupied. He was withdrawn from peers and with his teachers, he failed to show initiative, and was overly compliant. As the school year progressed, Ben had outbreaks of cruelty and aggressiveness toward other children with these being followed by episodes of confused speech that devolved into baby talk. Gross motor skills, which had earlier seemed within normal limits, deteriorated to the point where Ben's pediatrician worried about a possible neurological impairment, though none could be identified.

In his preschool classroom, Ben would sometimes stand immobile, staring into space for long periods and at other times he would dash off, crashing headlong into walls or furniture. At one point, he aggressively bit another child's fingers and became increasingly compelled to put objects into his mouth. When he behaved similarly at home and his parents would try to intervene, Ben responded with enraged temper displays accompanied by screaming and flailing about. He gouged scratches into his mother's arms and damaged walls and furniture.

Ben's teacher described how he would not protect himself from aggressively behaving peers, failing to protest or complain if others intruded into his space or bumped into him. In fact, he gravitated toward peers who were out of control. He made ugly gestures with his mouth then laughed as he told his teacher he was trying to scare her. At snack or lunch, he was upset by various foods and often gagged, saying he could only eat "soft things."

Through our work together, Ben's parents came to suspect that he had in some way been abused or traumatized. Increasingly, he brought questions and concerns to his parents about body parts, inquiring as to whether they could fall off. After his father helped him repair some damage to his room following a temper outburst, Ben confided in him and said, "When the bad man touched me, I tried to scare him off." Later, he was able to add more information, leading his parents to suspect that Ben had been molested at a park near their home while in the care of an inattentive babysitter. In response to this understanding and confronted with Ben's markedly disturbed behavior that would greatly interfere with his progress in kindergarten, the parents agreed to the recommendation for an analysis.

From the outset of the five-day-a-week treatment, it was evident that Ben's functioning was grossly impaired. He ignored the therapist and busied himself with compulsively counting or performing complicated math sums in his head. As he did this, he rocked back and forth, as if in a trance. Sometimes, he would pause in his recitations to make what seemed, on the surface, to be isolated comments. When he picked up and studied a crayon, he said his father had given him candy crayons for Easter. I said that I thought he might have been surprised by that. I commented that the office crayons were "just crayons" and reassured that I would try very hard to not make any surprises.

Ben began to draw pictures of monsters, calling them dinosaurs. In the pictures, there was fire all around. He drew big, penis-like hoses attached to the dinosaurs and explained that from them they squirted water onto the fires. Saliva went from their mouths, through their bodies, and out the hoses. Ben cautioned that if the hoses got too close to the fires, the flames could go into the dinosaurs' bodies and destroy them.

Ben noticed a coffee cup on my desk. He said his mother sometimes gave him coffee without caffeine. I said that I thought children felt safest when it was just their mothers who gave them things to eat and drink and Ben agreed.

During the next session, Ben seemed preoccupied and paced about the office, repetitively reciting TV commercials. Some were about cereal, some about soft drinks, and others about fast-food hamburgers. When I tried to speak to inquire, he would only chant louder, repeating then-popular "Big-Mac" and "RC Cola" commercials.

These repetitions continued for several days as he walked about the office, crashing his body into the furniture and walls, oblivious to all that was around him. I asked permission to offer a thought and when Ben allowed me to continue, I noted that all the commercials seemed to be about things to eat or drink. He said, "Right," and then grabbed up paper and pencil. Repeatedly, he drew a picture of a mouth and then cut it up with scissors.

Sometimes he would use tape to try to repair the cut-up circles and this progressed to covering his own mouth with layer upon layer of tape. After each layer was applied, he looked at his reflection in the base of a table lamp and then checked to see how much noise he could make from behind the tape. At no time would he allow me to talk, be it to offer a thought or ask a question.

After several days of this, Ben transitioned to folding a sheet of paper in half and aggressively cutting at it from the side. Then he would pause, open the paper, and look to see the resulting shape. Whenever it would be of a phallic-like design, he would smile and hold it to his mouth or place it between his legs. When he would finally allow me to inquire, I asked what he thought the shapes looked like. Ben then screamed the word "penis" and began to run around the room, shrieking, "The bad man's penis! The bad man's penis!"

I obtained Ben's permission to tell him that his parents had told me of how Ben had said there had been a bad man who had touched him and that he had tried to scare him off. Ben would not respond but looked sobered and returned to folding and cutting paper. As he did so, Ben found a small bottle of glue among the office supplies but could not use it beyond letting a few drops fall onto a piece of paper. As he did so, he seemed mesmerized. Abruptly, he became very excited and began to rip the paper and stuff it into his mouth. He screamed and jumped from the furniture. I asked if he was trying to let me know about something and he shouted, "The bad man put something sour in my mouth and it made me jump!"

Gradually, Ben was able to let himself hear my softly spoken words of sympathy as I said how terrible it must have been. He stopped jumping but continued to pace the office. He seemed comforted as I stressed how the bad time was in the past. Now, he had words to tell about it, so he could stop it from ever happening again.

Over the weeks and months that followed, Ben brought more material that helped us understand in greater detail the traumatic overwhelming he had suffered. Whenever the "bad man" was mentioned, Ben would dig at his bottom and say he needed to use the bathroom. As he walked down the hall to the restroom, his gait was stiff and awkward, and his toes turned inward. He wore his shorts so that his underwear protruded, and a large brown stain was visible. I gained his permission to say that it seemed he was trying to let me know something about what had happened when he was with the bad man. I observed that from the way he walked in the hallway, it looked as if his pants were full of bowel movement (bm). Ben seemed sad and sobered by this observation. I, too, felt this way and suspected that at the time of the molestation, Ben had lost control of his bowels, expelling them into his pants.

In similar fashion, Ben's behavior suggested other ways his body had responded to being overwhelmed. I began to suspect that he had lost control of his tears, his urine, and had also vomited. I first noted that, despite feeling overcome by sadness and upset, Ben struggled to prevent himself from crying during his sessions, furiously wiping away the tears as they approached. During this time, I learned from his parents that Ben had also regressed to wetting the bed at home each night, something that also caused him to feel very upset and unhappy. When I gained Ben's permission to let him know what his parents had told me, he burst into sobbing for several minutes. He was comforted by my words of sympathy. When the tears subsided, I connected again to the experience with the bad man. I said that while I couldn't know for sure, I wondered if his body had been letting us know that when it had happened, he'd lost control in so many ways; not only had his bm come out but that he'd cried and wet himself. Softly I said, "It must have seemed like your whole body was coming apart; you must have thought it would never end." Ben's response was to lie quietly and sadly on the couch till the end of the hour. A short time later, when visiting his pediatrician, Ben responded to a routine throat exam with fear and gagging. Later that day, during his session, Ben paced the room, gagging.

In a parent session later that week, Ben's mother and father described how Ben was acting afraid that he was going to vomit; he would cry and pace the floor at home complaining that he felt sick and worried that he might throw up. He was struggling to prevent it. When Ben could talk with me about this in his session, I said that wondered if the feeling he had felt with his doctor and the gagging that he'd later repeated in his session and at home, could be a way of letting us know that he might also have vomited when he'd been with the bad man. Ben agreed and then repeatedly recited the four things—his bm, urine, tears, and vomit—that had all come out of him during that terrible time.

Over the weeks and months that followed, the work with Ben took the form of constant and repetitive reworking of the molestation experience. Any transition in his life, such as entry into a new school grade, ushered in another reworking. He went through periods during which he would angrily deny there had ever been a molestation. It was important in the treatment to analyze this denial and see it as both a wish and a part of the working through process.

At one point, Ben tried to pinpoint the age he thought he must have been at the time he was abused. He determined that it must have happened a few months before his third birthday. This shortly preceded his entry into nursery school and corresponded with a time when his parents recalled having briefly used a sitter who later proved to be unreliable. Both Ben and his parents came to believe that the experience must have occurred at a time when Ben was still quite vulnerable to regression and when his limited language meant that he could not well communicate what had happened.

As time passed, Ben's aggressive conflicts remained especially pronounced and often interfered with forming friendships. Ben would become overly competitive and aggressive if he thought he might lose a game or have a toy taken from him. At the same time though, a tender side emerged, especially in his care of family pets and in his treatment of younger children.

Learning interferences persisted during the early elementary grades but eventually he came to earn A's and B's in his subjects.

The Case of Joey

Joey, another young child, entered five-times-per-week analysis at the age of four. During the analysis, it was determined that he had suffered a series of sexual abuse experiences at the hands of an elderly neighbor who had served as a frequent babysitter, before moving away from the neighborhood. This was a person toward whom Joey had felt warm and loving feelings, but these feelings became intermixed with angry excitement that was felt to be a consequence of the abuse, which had likely lasted over a period of several months, prior to the age of two-and-a-half.

Joey came to his analysis as a child compelled to repeat. He overwhelmed me with his words, even as he had felt overwhelmed. After referring to the neighbor, he would compulsively recite lists of all the things that caused him to worry. He was especially preoccupied with bathrooms, broken pipes, water, and floods. Over several weeks, he constructed pretend pipes made from scraps of paper that were held together by yards of tape. He said that pipes made him "think of mouths." When people threw up, things came out of their mouths like water out of a pipe. He reported frightening dreams of monsters with roaring mouths. All these thoughts reminded him of his old neighbor who had been his babysitter.

For several subsequent weeks, the play shifted to Joey constructing what he called a "dentist chair," covering both sides of piece of paper with dozens of bandages. Moments of contained work contrasted with times of acute anxiety as he talked of injuries he imagined happening to himself and to other family members.

With a fury, he brought his hurting fantasies into the transference. As his excited and worried thoughts escalated, he would hit, kick, and throw things at me. He tried to rub against me and pleaded with me to tickle him. He cried out that the neighbor had tickled him when babysitting for him. When he was able to calm a bit, I spoke to his boundary confusions—I was Dr. Barrett, not the old neighbor—and I softly repeated that now he was in a safe place where he could talk about what had happened without having to repeat it.

During the weeks that followed, Joey gradually sorted through the confused tangle of memories and feelings to give words to the terrible things that had occurred. He brought magazine cut-outs of a garden hose and held them close to my mouth. He excitedly said that hoses reminded him of penises and threw them about the room. While using glue, he was surprised when it squirted out of the bottle. He referred to it as "leaking out" and repeated the process several times. He tried to get into physical excitements with me and rushed to the waiting room to seek his mother's help to calm down. He told his mother that he was going back to tell me about his memories, "Real fast." He ran back into the office, threw himself on the couch, and showed again the tickling scenario. He tried to climb on my lap. Finally, he shouted that the neighbor had put a water bottle into his mouth and made him suck it. He cut up papers and threw them about the room. Again, he made glue leak out and rubbed against me and grabbed at me. When I reminded him that he could use his words, he ran to get his mother and brought her into the treatment room. There he told us both of how he'd seen liquid come from the man's penis and it looked like milk. The glue had reminded him of it.

After saying his mother could return to the waiting room, Joey referred to the dentist chair he'd made, calling it a "dangerous chair" because it made you, "lie down and open your mouth." He again ran at me to attack me and screamed, "I'll bite it again and again." He said, "C'mon," and threw himself back on the couch where he opened his mouth and said, "Ahhh." Finally, exhausted, he slumped and wondered how much time was left in the session. He said he was tired and wanted to sleep. I sat on a chair beside him and sympathized that it must have been terrible. I offered the thought that when it was over, he had wanted to sleep in hopes that his mom would come home soon. He softly said, "Yes."

The work that followed with Joey focused extensively on a defensive sexualization that resulted from what had occurred to him in a confusing relationship with a man that he both loved and hated. Joey was incapacitated by his excited, aggressive jealousy of others. It interfered with many aspects of his functioning but especially affected his relationships, school performance, and sports activities. We came to understand that his wish to bite off his neighbor's penis and have it as his own had become the prototype for his wish to have and incorporate anything he envied or desired. This wish was unconscious though, as was his terror of what his victims would do to him if they ever knew of his devouring jealousy. At a conscious level, all that appeared was a sabotaging of his efforts and activities. As Joey entered elementary school, he would anticipate and prepare for a sporting event, a project, or test at school only to have something happen to make him sick or injured, usually in some minor way but sometimes seriously.

A CONCLUDING THOUGHT

With cases of children who have been sexually abused at an early age, there are many defenses and connections back to the traumatic experience that need to be analyzed and reanalyzed to facilitate working through and ultimate integration. I stress this to illustrate it is the intensity and frequency of an analytic treatment that can be most effective, thus making analysis the treatment of choice for such children. Unlike a less frequent therapy, analysis best allows for access to the repressed, unconscious conflicts and fantasies. In my experience, it is also analysis that can best redress the atypical development that typically results from early trauma, offering the best support for an immature, developing ego as it struggles to gain relative mastery over what has occurred so that progressive development can be reattained.

NOTE

1. "The aversion to speak about trauma is a well-known phenomenon that is routinely reinforced by adults' failure to notice and their readiness to dismiss children's distress. Among abused and maltreated children, the taboo on speaking is compounded by the abuser's threats of terrible consequences if the child reveals what occurred. When the clinician does not discuss a traumatic occurrence, the child may conclude that the event is a forbidden topic and may hold on to the secret knowledge, wavering between fear of talking and hope that the clinician will signal permission to speak about the unspeakable" (Liberman & Van Horn, 2008).

Chapter Three

Developmental Consequences of Sexual Abuse

Christie Huddleston

Dr. Thomas Barrett's chapter provides us with a glimpse of his thoughtful clinical work with three children, all of whom had suffered significant sexual abuse by persons who were not immediate family members. In two cases, the abuse was part of a coercive, seductive process that occurred over months. In Ben's case, there was a single sexual assault by a stranger while under the care of an inattentive sitter. In each case, the child presented with difficult-to-explain symptoms of dysregulation such as sleep difficulties, eating issues, and problems around toileting and self-care. Also present were symptoms of developmental delay or frank regression and of disrupted ego functions. None of the children were able to connect his or her distress to the trauma they had experienced. The clinician had to listen carefully and attend to all levels of communication particularly nonverbal modes—closely attuned to their body language, somatic symptoms, and enactments—in order to aid the child's understanding of what was happening to them in the present and what had happened to them in the past; thus facilitating ego integration of the traumatic experience and reducing the push of the repetition compulsion.

In thinking about these three children and Dr. Barrett's work with them, I would like to discuss them in reverse order, starting with the youngest at the time of the abuse, since ego functioning is so much less mature for a two and a half to three-year-old child than that of a six to seven-year-old—the age at which Amy was abused. The developmental tasks of these phases of life are quite different also. In his chapter, Dr. Barrett makes the salient point that unrelated to the age the abuse occurs, it is not uncommon for sequelae to surface during adolescence with its hormonal upsurges, reworking of Oedipal conflicts, and second phase of individuation (Blos, 1967). Indeed, as in

Amy's case, she didn't come for help until she was a teenager in the throes of emotions that frightened and confused her. The fundamental experience of all children who are victims of physical or sexual abuse, including Dr. Barrett's patients, is the experience of an adult's misuse of them for the adult's purposes—the adult's intrapsychic and bodily needs—and the subsequent burden this puts on the child, mentally, physically, and developmentally. But what does this really mean? For the general public, there is a temptation to correlate the severity of the violence to the degree of psychological damage in the child. What happens during the abuse and the degree of violence matters, of course that is not all that matters. Many authors (Freud, 1895; Katan, 1961; Furman, 1956; Krystal, 1978; Shengold, 1980; Brenner, 2001) have written about the role of the psychological experience of the abuse and the subsequent meanings attached to it that are at least as threatening to the child's ego, and perhaps even at times, more so. In other words, as we know, the experience of the abuse itself may threaten annihilation and fracture the child's sense-of-self, mobilizing massive defenses of regression, repression, and dissociation; intolerable affects, intrusive ideation, unacceptable impulses, and superego attacks, all an inherent part of the psychological sequelae of abuse, will do the same. This raises technical issues for the clinician doing the necessary work of helping the child to know and integrate the traumatic experience so that the energies of the ego are freed up and forward development can proceed while trying not to retraumatize the child.

Dr. Barrett reports that Ben was less than three and Joey was less than two and a half years old when they were abused. Ben came to treatment at a younger age, most probably because his ego was profoundly overwhelmed by the violent assault on his small body resulting in periods of what I would think of as dissociated states alternating with aggressive outbursts. Both Ben and Joey seemed to have had reasonably normal development up until the time of the abuse, so we can assume they were navigating critically important tasks of toddlerhood in which the child develops a growing sense of self-awareness, strives for control of their bodies and bodily functions, and establishes greater independence from caregivers. Certain milestones have been reached. Toddlers are more mobile. They are verbal and engage in pretend play, demonstrating a nascent ability to symbolize and think about their broader world. Cognitively, they have moved into the preoperational mode of thinking. Still there is significant fragility to these advancements and the child remains highly dependent on the auxiliary ego of the parent. Katan (1961) noted that even though verbal, the toddler has not learned yet how to communicate his or her own inner emotional states or more abstract ideas. Fonagy et al. (2002) describe the child's thinking as egocentric and "naïve" and as having trouble distinguishing inner wishes from reality. Emphasizing the fragility of the toddler's growing independence, Mahler (1972) emphasized the emotionally charged, ambivalent nature of children toward their parents and other care-givers with the consequent anxiety of disruption in the relationship with their parents during the rapprochement subphase of the separation/individuation process. Marked by frequent meltdowns and temper tantrums, it is a confusing period for parents and children alike. Toddlers famously use the word "no" and oppositional behaviors not just to frustrate their parents—although the child's expression of aggression is an important part of this phase—but also to form and experience the boundaries of self and other. During rapprochement, libidinal development moves into the anal phase. The child learns to control the urethral and anal sphincters, allowing them to hold in body contents and eliminate them. Mastery of toileting is a source of pride and enhances a sense of self-control. Withholding and elimination provide sensual pleasure as well as serving aggressive functions. I am emphasizing here the child's ego as a body ego with an emphasis on the manner in which physical development and body experiences promote and inform psychological development (Freud, 1923), so that for toddlers, the maturation and control of the anal sphincter has an important contribution to the developing sense of self, self and object differentiation, emotional control, defenses of reaction formation, disgust, and identification with the aggressor (i.e., parental prohibitions and limits) and superego precursors of shame and pride—all major milestones of toddlerhood. Abuse during this period disrupts anal-phase development of the ego, heightens physiologically grounded aggression, amplifies ambivalence, creates distortions in reality testing, disrupts memory, and potentially fragments the sense of self processes detailed by Shengold (1989), Brenner (2001) and others. Abnormal defenses of denial, splitting, affective isolation or numbing, and dissociation, can also be mobilized.

We aren't given information about Joey's development prior to treatment or even his symptoms; however, we can see that Ben's development was disrupted by trauma. When he started preschool, which was thought to be shortly after the abuse, Ben was noted to be "unhappy, preoccupied, and distant from his peers." His teachers felt he was overly compliant. He stared off into space for long periods of time. Was this dissociation? Certainly, we could think of such a child as having a constricted ego (i.e., not having free access to vital energy which was bound up in defensively containing his instinctual impulses and intolerable affects). Later in the school year, these instinctual impulses began to break through his defenses and Ben would have "outbursts of cruelty and aggression toward other children and then regress into baby talk or crash into walls demonstrating heightened aggression and sadism toward self and others which his ego was unable to contain." At home, Ben would become enraged in the face of limits set by his parents and would damage furniture and walls, and attack his mother. I wonder if this reflected a confusion between the abuser and his parents in the moment of heightened emotions. One could also see a burgeoning sadomasochistic stance in his object relations. He sought peers who had poor impulse control but wouldn't protect himself. He tried to ward off his teacher by making scary faces at her. During what, I think, was an extended period of evaluation, Dr. Barrett reports that Ben was preoccupied with body parts and asked his parents repeatedly whether or not they could "fall off," revealing heightened castration fears. It was at this time that Ben was able to tell his father that "a bad man had touched" him. I think that Ben's ability to tell his father showed the value of the type of work that Dr. Barrett was offering and Ben's ability to use it. Dr. Barrett recommended analysis, and both Ben and his parents readily agreed.

Although a unique journey for each, the analyses of Ben and Joey exhibited elements of similarity. Ben started his analysis by ignoring the analyst and compulsively counting in his head, an anal defense of withholding, thus warding off the analyst and any dangerous stimulation from within or without. Joey accomplished warding off his analyst through a compulsive enactment in which he overwhelmed the analyst verbally, using a diarrhea of words. Intuitively, Dr. Barrett used his subjective experience to understand that Joey felt overwhelmed by the process of conveying his distress. Joey recited lists of his worries, including a preoccupation with bathrooms, broken pipes, water, and floods, the instinctual content of which seems to indicate concerns regarding castration—the broken pipe—and being flooded physically and psychically. Later in the analysis, we find that there are additional meanings to Joey's preoccupations, but, in the beginning, these are unknown. Like Ben, Joey seems to worry about his instinctual impulses, particularly his aggression and retaliatory castration. Joey makes "pretend pipes," taping scraps of paper together reparatively. Both Ben and Joey worry about monsters—a projection of their own rage. Joey's monsters roar in orally-tinged outrage, while Ben's monsters have large hose-like penises. These penises could squirt water to douse a fire but, Oh! The dinosaur must be careful not to get too close to the flame or his body would be consumed by the instinctual flame of passion!

Dr. Barrett sought to aid each of his patients in their worry about overstimulation and loss of ego control by emphasizing safety in the analytic hour. Ben talks of receiving candy crayons to eat from his father, while playing with analyst's crayons. I have to say I wondered if it were a screen memory for someone else's enticements. Dr. Barrett takes the opportunity to reassure Ben that his crayons are just ordinary crayons, not enticements and not to be eaten. Again, when Ben notes a coffee cup on his analyst's desk, he remarks that his mother sometimes gives him coffee. One can hear a kind of longing to be fed, to be given to, to share an intimacy with his analyst. In Ben's statement, Dr. Barrett understands these instinctual desires, but also how fraught this is for Ben. He responds by saying it is safest for children to eat and drink only what their mothers give them. Ben agreed. This statement must have offered some relief to Ben's confusion, confirming that the reality was that Dr. Barrett was not like the bad man who hurt him and the sense that his analyst knew how to keep him safe within his own internal world. This intervention seemed to provide Ben the sense of safety he needed to show his analyst more of what was on his mind as confusing as it was. Repetitions of jingles from food advertisements, alternating with periods of being in an altered state of consciousness in which he could not protect himself, signaled to his analyst the difficult analytic terrain he and his patient were on, and so the analyst asked permission to tell Ben about his—the analyst's—thoughts. Prior to this, Ben had blocked his analyst's attempts to communicate to him. Given a choice, which reinforced Ben's sense of agency, he then asked to know and his analyst shared that he had noticed Ben's chants were all about things to eat and drink. Then Ben was able to listen to what his analyst had on his mind and know more about what was on his own mind. He then used this knowledge and thinking together to further the interpretation through play mode. He drew a mouth and cut it up. He taped his own mouth shut and assessed how much could be heard through the tape. Was this a way of showing Dr. Barrett how his cries had been stifled at the time of the assault? And/or was it to express his deeply conflicted feelings about telling what had happened to him? He would not let his analyst speak during this time, demonstrating his need to pace the analysis to protect his sense of self and agency until he felt ready to proceed. He then began to cut paper, which at times had the shape of a penis. He would meaningfully put the paper to his mouth or between his legs. He smiled. In the moment was he thinking of his own penis? A friendly penis? Or, was the smile the frozen face of fear? Again, Dr. Barrett worked carefully, staying attuned to the cues and then asking Ben to verbalize what was being shown, letting him choose to say what was on his mind or not. Ben chose to reveal his thoughts to Dr. Barrett but in the telling, found himself in an overstimulated and unregulated state. He screamed the word "penis" and regressing to action mode began running around the room shrieking. Ben further elucidated his thoughts by blurting out, "It was the bad man's penis!" These moments must have been highly charged for Dr. Barrett as well as for Ben. Ben's sudden regression and dysregulation required intervention without moving away from the important content. Dr. Barrett reports speaking to Ben in softly spoken sympathetic words and tone which, I think, helped to modulate affects and therefore reinforced a sense of safety. With Ben's permission, Dr. Barrett repeated what Ben had told his parents about what the bad man had done. Why would this be important? Since splitting off of experience and denial of reality is such a pervasive defense after traumatic events, I believe Dr. Barrett did not assume that Ben could remember what he told his parents in any continuous and integrated memory, therefore Dr. Barrett was bringing the memory into the dyad to hold for and with Ben as he gained the capacity to think about the traumatic events and bear the feelings attached to them. Dr. Barrett then interpreted to Ben that now he had words and could protect himself from assault. This marked a turning point in their work together. Through play, Ben was able to show Dr. Barrett that he had lost control of bodily functions during the assault, and Dr. Barrett put this into words for Ben. There was a long working through process in which Ben would deny the abuse periodically. Dr. Barrett understood this in two ways: (i) a wish that it had never happened and, (ii) as a part of the working-through process. With this work, Ben more actively collaborated with Dr. Barrett.

In his analysis, Joey seemed to be aware that his dreams and worries of pipes, mouths, and monsters were related in some way to his older neighbor who had cared for him and for whom he had markedly ambivalent feelings. In play, he constructed a dentist chair and worried about injuries to himself and family. His feelings toward the neighbor moved forcefully into the transference so that Dr. Barrett became the hated and feared seducer. Joey would hit, kick, and throw things at his analyst and then beg for his analyst to tickle him. This is a not uncommon aspect of the repetition compulsion in which the child sexualizes their relationships with others. Shengold (1989) speaks of the mismatch of the adult's sexuality to that of a child's, writing that,

> A child's sexual excitement in relation to an adult's cannot result in any kind of balanced mutuality; it is simply too much for the child, whose psychosexual organization is not capable of adequate discharge in orgasm. The wish for, the need for discharge is expressed through the child's fainting . . . but a full release cannot be achieved . . . the wish for an explosive penetration . . . can be mobilized to end the torment of prolonged unbearable forepleasure. (p. 61)

The child's relative inability to discharge intense sexual feeling leads to a push to master overstimulation by recreating similar experiences in the hope that there will be a kind of discharge and relief. As this intense transferential manifestation occurred early in the analysis, Dr. Barrett chose to address Joey's confusion of past and present reality by emphasizing that he was not the neighbor. Subsequently, Joey was able to confirm that his neighbor had tickled him as part of the abuse. As Joey progressed in his analysis, like Ben, he too spoke of penis-like hoses and held them to the analyst's mouth. He too was drawn to the glue in his analyst's office. It reminded him of things "leaking out," and he linked this to memories of his neighbor. He then returned to his construction of the dentist chair further elaborating by calling it the "dangerous chair" because it "made you lie down and open your mouth" and integrating his memories of being coerced sexually. This was not without great cost. He suffered moments of intense anxiety, dysregulation, and rage. He attacked Dr. Barrett screaming, "I'll bite you," and invited Dr. Barrett to put his penis in his mouth. He then collapsed in exhaustion, thus shutting down the emotional storm accompanying the reconstruction—or is it really a construction of the abuse—with his analyst.

Amy, in her early teens, presented for treatment after an emotional storm of a whole other level of risk. While home, she erupted in a burst of anger, verbally castigating a close friend. Immediately, feeling enormous guilt, she attacked herself with a razor, cutting her wrists so deeply that it required ten stitches to close the wound. No superficial scratching was this. Usual wrist-slashing seen in the emergency room requires a few sterostrips, antibacterial ointment, and a referral for suicidal evaluation. What provoked this outburst? We are told that Amy had been hanging out with friends on a day off from school when her girlfriend spilled paint making a mess that, for some reason, was intolerable for Amy. Experiencing an upsurge of emotions that she seemed to have been unaware of, she acted impulsively and destructively. Witnessing this, her friends screamed in horror.

Dr. Barrett states that Amy's physical appearance at the beginning of their work seemed to convey an edgy, divided sense of herself. Notable was her excitement in acknowledging that her friends "freaked out" when she forced them to witness her cutting. I wondered if an important part of this enactment was a voyeuristic satisfaction derived from watching them feel a disavowed feeling of her own demonstrating an identification with the aggressor, in this case an abusive older boy. This boy was the son of a man Amy's mother had dated and lived with after the divorce with Amy's father. The boy, age thirteen, was enlisted to babysit Amy when she was six or seven years old. The abuse continued some months until Amy told her mother. Fortunately, Amy's mother believed her and relinquished the relationship with her boyfriend, ending the abuse from his son. It may have been that her mother was hoping such concrete steps would be enough to prevent Amy from any psychological sequelae, as she did not seek treatment for Amy at the time. Dr. Barrett reports that during the abuse, Amy was symptomatic for nightmares and sleepwalking, which propelled Amy to sleep most nights with her mother. She also developed an enlarged colon, which, I agree with Dr. Barrett, probably represents an attempt to contain and control her overwhelming feelings through a physiologic withholding.

At the time of the sexual abuse, Amy would normally have been in the phase of early latency. In normal development, the child of early latency lives in the shadow of the Oedipal phase under threat of the instincts breaking through repression. New to triadic relatedness with its genital and romantic strivings, jealousy and fear of retribution, the child has gained important internal resources for self-regulation through superego formation. Although over time, the superego will become more modulated, the superego of early latency is harsh and punitive. In latency, instinctual breakthrough is at first met by this harsh superego but over time, the ego develops a higher order system of defenses and fantasies to express and defend against Oedipal and pre-Oedipal instincts (Sarnoff, 1971). With greater control of their instinctual life, the child can look outward to the world-at-large socially and intellectually participating in full-day school, peer relationships, and group activities. Aggressive or sexual overstimulation destabilizes or delays this maturational process and the individual is left with a variety of psychological fault lines: inadequate fusion of drives, less flexibility of defenses, and over-reliance on a harsh superego.

With the advent of hormonal, psychological, and social pressures, girls in early adolescence, such as Amy, are thrust into a reworking of early maternal-child bonds, and anal conflicts around messiness and self-care because of the experience of menstruation. Indeed, Dr. Barrett wondered if the impulsive cutting provoked by her girlfriend's "messiness" was in part related to Amy's having recently attained menarche as well as to the absence of her mother from the home. "Messiness" also seemed directly linked to the abuse and Amy's experience of her sitter's ejaculations. Dr. Barrett notes certain elements of Amy's personality also seem to reflect residue from the earlier abuse such as her interest in experiencing feelings of fear and horror in books and movies as an attempt at mastery of these feelings, but perhaps also, like Joey, as a longing for a sexualized excitement. Dr. Barrett notes that Amy had already had multiple short-lived romantic liaisons with boys, which to my mind would seem another attempt to both seek out and master fear laden and overwhelming sexual feelings.

In summary, Dr. Barrett has given us a clear picture of the effects of sexual abuse as it impacts children of different phases of development and of different genders. He discusses the immediate impact of such abuse and the long-term sequelae in personality development. More importantly, he helps us to think about how to approach the myriad of difficult feelings and thoughts these children would present to any clinician. He emphasizes certain aspects of his analytic techniques which he feels facilitates the child's engagement with the analyst in the face of overwhelming feelings, disorganization, memory difficulties, and intense transferential experiences.

Chapter Four

Be Careful What You Wish For!

The Seduction of Adolescent Males by Female Teachers

Calvin A. Colarusso
with an addendum by Gordon Caras

During the course of their adolescent years, most students, male and female, develop crushes on their teachers. Psychoanalytic developmental theory understands the role of those crushes in furthering separation/individuation and integrating physical and psychological sexual maturity. However, in the three cases that I will present, teenage crushes were not what started the sexually abusive relationships. In each instance, the teacher was the instigator and the aggressor.

Most adolescent males and their adult counterparts are only too happy to discuss their sexual fantasies about one or more teachers who were the object of their sexual and masturbatory fantasies. What is more macho than bragging to your buddies about thinking about, or actually having sex with a teacher? Most boasts are just empty bravado, intended to impress others, and bolster adolescent insecurities; but in some instances, it really happened. What a conquest! What a way to be a big man on campus!

Through the presentation of three forensic case studies, I will describe the very traumatic psychological and emotional consequences that resulted from these relationships. Yes indeed, be careful what you wish for! In addition to describing the three case histories, in my discussion of the effect of the sexual abuse on these three adolescents, I will make reference to relevant psychoanalytic developmental theory to provide a framework of normality against which to compare and discuss the harmful effects of these relationships on the students. My intent in this contribution is to present unique clinical material that is not in the psychiatric or psychoanalytic literature and to describe the traumatic effects of such encounters on adolescent development and psychopathology. Although legal proceedings are part of the public record, I have gone to great lengths to protect the confidentiality of the students and the perpetrators. I could not find any references in the psychoanalytic literature to sexual abusive relationships between adult female teachers and adolescent male students. I will now present the three case histories.

JACK

I was asked to do a child psychiatric evaluation of Jack, as we will call him, and serve as an expert witness in his lawsuit, by his attorney. When Jack was thirteen years of age, he was abused by a female teacher. The perpetrator had been tried and convicted. My evaluation consisted of an interview with Jack's mother and a separate one with him. In addition, psychological testing was administered by a forensic psychologist of my choosing; and multiple records were reviewed, including the police report, indictment, sentencing, and probation requirements.

Diagnostic Interview with Mother

All of the following information was obtained directly from Jack's mother. No one else was present during the interview. Mother was informed that this was not a doctor/patient relationship and there was no confidentiality; lawyers from both sides would have access to my chart. Mother was a single parent working as a clerk to support her children. Jack's father was in jail. The couple never married and the father never lived with his son. Jack asked to meet his father, who lived in the area, when the boy was ten-years-old. The visit was their first and last contact. Jack recently became a father himself. He, his girlfriend, and infant child lived with his mother.

Mother found out about her son's involvement with the perpetrator, whom we will call Mrs. L., a woman in her thirties, when the teacher reported her car stolen. The police investigated and implicated Jack and an older boy. During the investigation, Jack told the authorities that he had not stolen the car: Mrs. L let him drive it in exchange for sex.

Mrs. L. gave Jack and other students alcohol. She also called the school, disguising her voice, and said that it was okay for Jack to walk home; thus allowing them to spend time together. Mother discovered through her lawyer that Jack had had sex with Mrs L. in mother's home. When asked, mother had no difficulty describing the changes that were evident in her son during and after the sexual abuse ended: "He wants to be the boss, the man." Displaying empathy for Jack, she said, "He was only thirteen, he didn't understand. He's embarrassed about it. He told me that every time he thinks of it, he feels like throwing up."

Jack is trying to straighten up. After the abuse was discovered, he became angry and began drinking heavily. Jack lost respect for women. Now he has stopped drinking and is planning to graduate from high school. He saw a social worker for about eighteen months on a weekly basis but was not in therapy at the time of this evaluation. He had not had any prior therapy.

Developmental History

Mother had no problems during the full-term pregnancy. She did not use drugs or alcohol. Labor and delivery occurred without complication. Jack was bottle-fed and weaned at one year. Early developmental milestones occurred at expected intervals. He was a happy baby and toddler who was toilet trained easily in the second and third year of life. There were no major separations from mother. Jack did well in kindergarten.

In third grade, though, Jack was suspended after another student put a knife in his backpack. His interest in school waned after that. Jack's sixth grade teacher suggested that he be held back so he could catch up academically. Jack played Little League baseball and Pop Warner football and was happy at home. He has not had any major illnesses or operations in his life. After Jack met his father when he was ten, he frequently asked to see him again. Mother tried to arrange future meetings, but father wasn't interested.

Puberty occurred at age twelve to thirteen. Jack accepted the changes easily. The sexual relationship with Mrs. L. started shortly after Jack went through puberty. Mrs. L. introduced Jack to alcohol. He denied using drugs.

During his freshman year in high school, Jack and one of his friends broke into a neighbor's home. As a result, he spent three months in juvenile hall. The neighbor spoke up for Jack and blamed the intrusion on alcohol use and Jack's older friend. Recently, a neighbor called the police because underage drinking was taking place at a neighborhood family party. When the police arrived, Jack and a friend ran. Jack ordered a man on a bike to get off and not look back. He was placed on probation for a second time for that offense.

Diagnostic Interview with Jack

I saw Jack shortly before his eighteenth birthday. He looked like an adult man in his twenties and was pleasant and cooperative and talked readily about himself and his experiences. I asked about his girlfriend and infant child, who were in the waiting room during the interview. Jack met his girlfriend through a cousin. She became pregnant while both were drunk a few weeks after they met. The couple decided to keep the child and began to live with Jack's mother.

Jack attends high school and plans to graduate. He wants to succeed and buy a house. The couple plans to marry in a few years if they are still together. Jack described his child as "happiness." He enjoys taking care of the baby. Living with mother is difficult because the couple doesn't have much privacy. Jack hopes to get his high school diploma by the end of the summer and then work in construction.

When asked, Jack told me about Mrs. L. in a matter of fact way. He didn't seem embarrassed. In fact, I had to remind myself that I was talking to a seventeen year old boy. Jack met Mrs. L at school. Everyone knew that she gave students alcohol. Mrs. L. took an immediate interest in Jack. They began to talk in the hallway. She told Jack about her life. Things were not good with her husband. She wanted a divorce. Jack talked of the meager finances at home and his desire to party. Because he knew that Mrs. L. had provided alcohol to students, he asked if she would buy some for him.

Jack asked for Mrs. L.'s phone number, which she provided readily. Before they parted, his teacher pulled Jack's face into her breasts. When she did that, Jack knew that she was interested in him sexually. When Jack called Mrs. L. soon afterwards, he suggested that she come to his home because his mother was working. On the phone, before she came over, thirteen-year-old Jack asked if they could try it, meaning have sex. He had a condom, obtained from an older friend.

Soon after Mrs. L. arrived, she gave Jack oral sex and then got on top of him and had intercourse. Jack was a virgin. He was curious about intercourse. He was not in love with Mrs. L., but he felt something for her.

Over the course of the next year, in her car and at her home, they had intercourse and oral sex approximately thirty times. Sometimes Jack did not use a condom. He felt that Mrs. L. seemed to like him a lot. Once at Mrs. L.'s home, a teenage girl who was there showed an interest in Jack. They were on their way to make out when Mrs. L. stopped them.

Jack told two of his friends a few years older than he, that he was having sex with his teacher. When Jack introduced his friends to Mrs. L., she had intercourse with both boys. After the relationship with Mrs. L. ended, Jack had sex with approximately eight different girls. None of these girls became pregnant.

As I had with his mother, I asked Jack how he felt the relationship with Mrs. L. had affected him.

"She made me feel older. She let me drive her car and bought me beer and clothes. She made me feel like a man."

"I developed a drinking problem. We always drank first. She would buy two thirty-packs of beer." Jack often drank ten beers when they were together. After meeting Mrs. L., Jack began to drink regularly. This pattern continued after their relationship ended. He stopped drinking after discovering that he was going to become a father. Jack has not had anything to drink since, understanding that he can't drink because he loses control.

"She gave me money, $300. She made me feel older. She gave me the $300 after we had been meeting for two to three months. I used it to buy beer and gas."

Jack was embarrassed after his family learned what had happened. In addition, he was teased by his friends because Mrs. L. was older and not very good looking. When the sexual abuse became public, Jack's name was not mentioned in the newspaper. He tries not to think about it. Jack volunteered that he wished he knew his father "to learn about being a man. He never accepted me."

On mental status examination, Jack presented as a casually dressed, late-adolescent. He was calm and cooperative throughout the diagnostic interview. Jack had an average English vocabulary. His affect was calm and euthymic as he talked about the sexual involvement with Mrs. L. Thinking was logical and goal directed, and the adolescent was oriented as to time, person, and place. He interpreted proverbs abstractly.

Review of Records

The complaint described the inappropriate sexual behavior between a John Doe and the defendant Mrs. L. The indictment described multiple counts against Mrs. L., including sexual intercourse and oral sex with a minor. Court records included the pretrial evaluation, imposition of sentence, presentencing report and the rules of detention. Mrs. L was sentenced to six months in jail, ten years of probation, and a requirement to register as a sex offender.

Psychological Testing

A battery of psychological tests was administered, at my request, by an experienced forensic psychologist. His findings are summarized here.

The CBRS, Comprehensive Behavioral Rating Scales, is an assessment tool used to obtain a parent's observations about their child's behavior. Mother's assessment of her son suggests that Jack has significant problems in the areas of anxiety, depression, defiance, aggressive behaviors, perfectionistic and compulsive behaviors, and separation fears.

"Diagnostic impressions of both mood and behavioral disorder are supported by this instrument."

Jack was administered the Shipley 2, a brief measure of cognitive functioning and impairment. "His performance on this instrument, when considered in relation to his reported history, suggests problems with attention and concentration. Overall, it would appear that Jack is of low average intelligence with some evidence of attention and concentration problems."

The TSCC, Trauma Symptom Checklist for Children, is a self-report measure of post-traumatic distress. Jack demonstrates no clinically significant elevations on any of the scales on this instrument.

The SASSI-A2, Substance Abuse Subtle Screening Inventory, Adolescent Version, 2nd Edition, is designed to accurately discriminate between adolescents who have a problem with substance abuse and those who do not. "Jack openly admits having problems with alcohol that include drinking during the day, drinking more than he intended to, and getting into trouble because of his drinking, all several times each. He denies any history of other drug use. He responds to the SASSI-A2 in a manner that indicates he has a low probability of having a substance abuse diagnosis."

The PAI-A, Personality Assessment Inventory, Adolescent Version, 2nd Edition, is a self-report, objective measure of psychopathology and personality functioning in adolescents. "His PAI-A profile is marked by a significant elevation on a measure of alcohol abuse. He reports that his use of alcohol has had a negative impact on his life. Alcohol-related problems are likely, including difficulties in his interpersonal relationships, difficulties at school, and legal complications."

"The minor's self-concept is rather negative."

"Beneath his cooperative and controlled façade are marked feelings of personal inadequacy and insecurity that are evident in his tendency to put himself down, magnify his weaknesses and limitations, and anticipate rejection."

"Jack expresses concerns about issues related to sexuality. He harbors reservations about his sexual behavior as well as a sense of confusion or discontent in relation to his impulses and interests, and the roles he is expected to assume. Troubled by these feelings, he may restrain his romantic inclinations until he is able to clarify his current feelings."

The psychologist suggested the following diagnostic possibilities on DSM-4: generalized anxiety disorder and alcohol abuse by history. On Axis II, he noted compulsive and dependent personality traits. On Axis IV, he listed the molestation by Mrs. L. The psychologist rated Jack's symptoms in the moderate range of severity.

Diagnosis

The Diagnostic and Statistical Manual of the American Psychiatric Association is the only used diagnostic nomenclature in the field. I recognize that it is not dynamically oriented, but it is simple, descriptive and the standard in both civil and criminal court proceedings. The fourth edition was in use at the time of this evaluation. Using that framework, I made the following diagnoses in regard to Jack.

Axis I: Sexual Abuse of Child V61.21; 995.53, indicating clinical attention is on the victim. (I am aware that sexual abuse is a V. Code and not a formal diagnosis). Alcohol Dependence 303.90, Early Full Remission.

Axis II: Both clinical evidence and psychological testing data indicate the presence of compulsive and dependent personality traits.

Axis III: No medical conditions of significance were present.

Axis IV: Psychosocial and Environmental Problems:

- Problems with primary support group—absence of a father or father figure.
- Educational problems—academic problems, discord with teachers and classmates.
- Economic problems—significant economic deprivation, difficulty supporting self, girlfriend, and son.
- Problems related to interaction with the legal system/crime: litigation, victim of crime, history of probation.

Axis V: Global Assessment of Functioning: I rated Jack's symptoms in the 41–50, serious range.

Treatment and Prognosis

This young man obviously has multiple emotional problems that predated the sexual abuse by his teacher. Treatment recommendations and costs are a part of determining and awarding damages in civil law suits. Thus, the following recommendations are meant to indicate what I felt was required to treat his sexual and alcohol related issues that resulted from the sexual abuse by his teacher.

I recommended individual psychotherapy, twice per week, for two years; and in the decade following the completion of the first course of psychotherapy, an additional interval of individual psychotherapy, once per week for two years. Antianxiety medication may be helpful during the course of therapy. I considered the prognosis for recovery from the effects of the sexual abuse to be fair to good.

Summary

Jack was thirteen to fourteen when he was sexually abused by Mrs. L. He was stimulated by the reports of classmates that Mrs. L. would obtain alcohol for students. When Mrs. L. made sexual references and advances, Jack quickly responded due to his curiosity. Their sexual involvement, which included oral sex and intercourse, occurred more than thirty times.

The experiences, although clearly exciting and pleasurable physically, had a significant negative effect on Jack's self-esteem and led to a drinking problem, which is now in remission. The hypersexuality that developed at the beginning of adolescence led to his numerous, impulsive sexual encounters with girls and the pregnancy that resulted from the drunken sex that Jack engaged in with his girlfriend of two weeks. Now, not yet eighteen, he is a father, and any chances for a carefree adolescence during which he would have had time to develop mentally, emotionally, sexually, and educationally are gone. These experiences and their consequences will continue to have a significant effect on his mental and emotional state for years to come.

ANDREW

Andrew was sixteen years old when I was asked by his attorney to serve as a child psychiatric expert in his lawsuit against his teacher. I had two diagnostic interviews with his parents and saw Andrew three times. In addition, a complete battery of psychological tests was administered by an experienced forensic psychologist, and I reviewed multiple records. Fortunately, I was able to refer Andrew to a child analyst for treatment. He was kind enough to prepare a summary of his treatment of Andrew, which will be presented later.

First Diagnostic Interview with Andrew

Although Andrew was sixteen years old at the time of our meeting, he looked more like a twenty-five or thirty-year-old adult. Towering over me, at approximately six feet, five inches, his shy, anxious demeanor was totally incongruous with his appearance. Following standard, psychoanalytical practice in the evaluation of adolescents, I saw Andrew before I interviewed his parents in order to establish a rapport and express my respect for him as an individual.

I began the interview by explaining to Andrew about the nature of our relationship and the absence of confidentiality. Following questions about his family and his interests that were asked to allow him to relax and to establish a nonthreatening rapport, I asked Andrew to describe the relationship with his teacher in his own words, in any order that felt comfortable. Andrew lived in an intact family with his parents and siblings in a comfortable, middle class home.

Andrew began by talking about school. He has seven classes, including four advanced placement classes, and has a cumulative GPA of 3.85. Andrew played varsity sports in his sophomore year but decided not to play during the current school year because of what happened with his teacher. There was just too much talk about it at school. The adolescent's life was centered on his studies and video games. Andrew slept anywhere from four to ten hours a night, often studying until morning. He used to have close friends and had been dating a very popular girl, but all that changed after the scandal. Despite his size and appearance, Andrew described himself as immature. His parents wanted him to excel academically. He would like to go to an Ivy League college but had not yet decided on a major.

Without prompting, he volunteered information about his teacher. Mrs. Q. was in her forties when she taught Andrew in ninth grade. She put her hand on his shoulder and said that rules didn't apply to him because he was more mature than the other students. Andrew was not physically attracted to Mrs. Q. but enjoyed the attention.

Andrew had experienced puberty during fifth-grade and had had intercourse for the first time during his freshman year, before involvement with Mrs. Q. He regretted the initial experience of sex because it wasn't with someone special; the girl had come on to him, as many girls did. During his sophomore year, he had sex with his girlfriend and two other girls.

Mrs. Q. created a Twitter account and sent Andrew a private message that included her phone number. She said if he ever needed *anything*, he should call her. Mrs. Q. began to flirt, calling him "baby" and "sweetheart." One day after football practice, Mrs. Q. was waiting for Andrew and asked him to get in the car. Andrew said that prior to actually being alone with Mrs. Q., he had flirted back. But this was a "little too much." In the car, Mrs. Q. talked about her attraction to Andrew and said that she had a husband and could get into trouble if they were caught together.

Continuing to tell his story with mild pressure of speech and some embarrassment, Andrew then mentioned that his teacher showed up at one of his basketball games. She became "abnormally excited." Mrs. Q. had talked to Andrew's mother at the game, telling her that she had been tutoring Andrew. That wasn't true. Mrs. Q. texted Andrew and told him that he would get "extra credit" for playing so well.

Soon after, Mrs. Q. sent nude photos of herself. Andrew reemphasized that he was not physically attracted to her. She asked him to send her a picture "of my dick." Andrew had never done that before and didn't think he should but was excited by the idea. He showed the nude pictures of Mrs. Q. to his buddies. They were very impressed and told him to "go for it."

Then, at a basketball game, Mrs. Q. got in Andrew's car and told him to drive. They went to a private area behind a store. Mrs. Q. touched Andrew's leg in the car and started kissing him. She opened his pants, grabbed his penis, and began sucking it. Andrew did not have a full erection and did not ejaculate despite the fact that the oral sex went on for forty-five minutes. Andrew tried to become aroused by thinking about the other girls that he had had sex with. Mrs. Q. said that Andrew's penis was bigger than her husband's. "I felt uncomfortable." He suggested that they return to the basketball game. Afterward, Andrew told his friends what had happened and gave them Mrs. Q.'s Twitter account password.

After rumors of Andrew's involvement with Mrs. Q. spread through the school, he was called to the principal's office and asked if there had been any physical contact with Mrs. Q. When Andrew said no, the principal let him go back to class and did not notify his parents or call the police. Later, when the police became involved, they asked Andrew to write a detailed statement of what happened. Mrs. Q. had told Andrew that if their relationship became public, she would kill him or kill herself.

"I believed that she would kill herself."
"I'd be driving and see an older woman and put her face" (on the person).
"I was scared she was casing my house."
"I had nightmares of her coming after me."
"I dreamt about her blowing me up."

Andrew also had dreams of Mrs. Q. poisoning his coffee. These thoughts and feelings were still present at the time of the evaluation. Indeed, they had "become more frequent. I can't sleep anymore."

A few days before our session, Andrew saw a woman on the street and thought it was Mrs. Q. "I thought I had a hallucination."

"She's scary. She really is!"
"I'm afraid to go to school!"
"People say, 'how can you be scared of her, you're so big?'"
"She's just a little woman. She really is scary. I'm afraid of crazy people."
When he talked, the seventeen-year-old sounded more like a child.

Diagnostic Interviews with Andrew's Parents

After informing the parents that I was serving as an expert witness in their lawsuit, I verified the identifying information provided by Andrew and asked them to tell me their understanding of the relationship between Andrew and his teacher.

Upon interviewing Andrew at school, a detective called mother and told her that her child had been a victim of sexual abuse by an adult. At school, Andrew and his parents met with the school principal and two detectives. Andrew had refused to give his phone number or talk to the detectives by himself. He initially denied having a sexual relationship with Mrs. Q.

Then, the detectives informed the parents of a video on Andrew's phone that pictured him having sex with his teacher. The night before the meeting with the authorities again, Andrew confessed to his father. He told his mother the next day. After meeting with the school officials and detectives, father contacted an attorney.

The parents described their son's reactions to the involvement with Mrs. Q.

Andrew lost twenty-five pounds after the sexual abuse was revealed. At the same time, he developed severe acne and picked at his face. In retrospect, the acne began about the time that Mrs. Q. was attempting to seduce Andrew. His parents recalled seeing Mrs. Q. at all of the basketball games. They thought that was odd but had no idea what was happening.

Andrew usually slept like a log growing up. But in the months prior to the discovery of the sexual abuse, their son would come home from school and go to sleep. He often skipped dinner and then got up at midnight and stayed up all night. The loud music that he played caused the neighbors to complain. "I only find peace at night," he said.

Father said that Andrew only felt safe when someone else was home to protect him. One evening, father returned home from a trip at night. Andrew heard a noise and attacked his father in the dark, thinking that he was an intruder.

"Andrew is living in fear that she will kill him."

After the sexual abuse became public, Andrew began carrying a bat and a knife in his car. He had a machete in his room. Andrew's fear also extended to Mrs. Q.'s husband and relatives. He urged his father to buy a gun. Andrew began to stay overnight at friends' homes because he thought that Mrs. Q. could not find him there.

In addition, he let his hair and beard grow. To his parents' dismay, Andrew went to school dressed in pajamas and a hoody. Before the involvement with Mrs. Q., he was "all about fashion." Their son was "the coolest kid in the school. He was a star." Now he was changed.

"I don't want anyone to notice me. I want to disappear."
"I don't want to date anyone. I just want to study."
"I know I look like a man, but I'm a boy."

The family's cars were broken into several times. Used tampons were left on the hood of Andrew's car. Their home was egged.

Andrew became very cruel toward his mother. He called her "disgusting" and said she smelled. Andrew said that he hated her and accused her of cheating on her husband. Recently, he pushed his mother who hurt her arm when she fought back. The verbal attacks on mother occurred every time father left on business. Andrew's fears definitely increased when father was away. Andrew reported repeated nightmares in which he was killed by Mrs. Q.

The day before I met with his parents, Andrew said that he was going to kill himself. He often talked about dying young. Two days ago, in a severely fearful, paranoid state, Andrew told a friend that his teacher was outside and was coming after him. Mrs. Q. continued to threaten Andrew on Instagram.

At a judicial hearing regarding Mrs. Q.'s sentence, it was revealed that there were at least two, and possibly four other victims.

Developmental History

I obtained the following developmental history from the parents. Andrew was delivered after a full-term pregnancy. Mother had prenatal care throughout the pregnancy and did not take drugs or use alcohol. Andrew weighed eight pounds at birth. He was breastfed for two years. Mother was his primary caretaker. Developmental milestones occurred on time or were early. Andrew was toilet trained easily but occasionally wet the bed until second grade. There were no significant separations from either parent during the first five or six years of life.

During latency, Andrew separated easily to go to school. He was well-behaved and had many friends. His primary interest was sports. The family spent evenings and weekends together and took vacations, mainly to visit relatives.

Puberty occurred at age eleven. Andrew began dating during his early teen years and became sexually active in high school. In junior high school, Andrew made the honor roll and had a GPA of 3.8. He played basketball until the sexual abuse occurred. When he quit, Andrew told his parents he stopped because he was jeered and teased after what happened with Mrs. Q. became public.

"His attitude toward women has changed."
"Girls on the campus called him 'asshole Andrew'"
He didn't go to the prom.

Second Diagnostic Interview with Andrew

I asked Andrew to tell me in his own words how he felt he was affected by his relationship with Mrs. Q. His anxiety was palpable as he volunteered much of the following without prompting.

"I'm very anxious in school."
"I freak out if I see an older woman. Is it Mrs. Q.?"
"I have nightmares. There are one million ways in which she kills me."
"I check my car every time I get in it."
"Other teachers are being nice to me. It's upsetting. One female teacher, after she found out gave me a hug. It made me anxious."
"I'm always looking for her and her family. I met some of her relatives. They are big. They're going to come after me."
"I look in my rearview mirror all the time."

Andrew experienced heavy breathing and was nauseated in school. He walked around school with his headphones on and his head down.

Andrew has dreams in which he turns on the radio and the car blows up. In other dreams, someone chokes him or shoots at him. Very often it is Mrs. Q. herself. She hits him. He tries to fight back but can only move in slow motion. Andrew also daydreams that some member of her family will shoot him.

At the time of the diagnostic evaluation, it had been approximately thirteen months since the oral sex occurred. After that experience, things were "normal for a while" as Andrew avoided Mrs. Q. and spent time with his friends. Occasionally, Mrs. Q., would send a text message. Andrew would not reply. These messages were not sexual in nature. She usually asked how things were going. Once or twice, Mrs. Q. sent a picture of herself.

Then, at the beginning of the current school year, Mrs. Q. was friendly and asked how school was going. They saw each other more frequently because both were involved in a school organization that collected money for the athletic programs after sporting events. One evening after a sporting event, Andrew was sitting in his car in the parking lot with the door open. Mrs. Q. insisted on going with Andrew to pick up the money that had been collected. "She was scary." She asked about "last year," referring to the fellatio. Andrew tried to avoid answering. Mrs. Q. asked about his plans for college.

As the fall progressed, Mrs. Q. began texting again. She said that she was glad that he was back, "Like we broke up." Mrs. Q. asked Andrew to add her to his Snapchat account. She sent nude pictures and invited him over. One weekend, Mrs. Q. insisted that Andrew come to her home. No one would be at home until six in the evening. When he resisted, she asked him to get some marijuana for her. Andrew agreed and went to her house to pick up the money to buy the pot. When he arrived, Mrs. Q. got into his car and went with him to pick up the marijuana. After getting the pot, she insisted they return to her house.

Once there, Mrs Q. took Andrew into the house and pushed a drink on him. Over the space of approximately thirty minutes, he drank five shots of whiskey. Mrs. Q. texted her husband to find out the time he would be home. While taking Andrew on a tour of the house, Mrs. Q. grabbed his crotch. He was standing in her bedroom at the time. He told her that the blinds were open, then got up and went downstairs. On the way down, Mrs. Q. told Andrew that she was unhappy with her husband and it was his fault.

Mrs. Q. jumped on the kitchen counter and told Andrew to have intercourse with her. He mentioned that people would see them and was reluctant. Mrs. Q. closed the blinds and took off her clothes. When Andrew said it was not a good idea, Mrs. Q. pulled his pants down to his knees and gave him oral sex for several minutes. Then the teacher wrapped her legs around him and they had intercourse. Andrew did not use a condom and pulled out before ejaculating. He took a video in order to prove to his friends that he had sex with her.

"I could have stopped it, but I didn't."

Mrs. Q. warned Andrew, "If you tell anyone, I swear to God, I'll freaking kill you."

Andrew put his clothes on and ran out the side door. He was scared. Feeling both exhilarated and apprehensive, Andrew called a friend and went to his house and showed him the video. He smelled of alcohol. Two other friends were there and they also saw the video. The group drove to another friend's house where the video was again shown. Andrew bragged that he had sex with Mrs. Q. but also told his friends that she said she was going to kill him. Two of the friends who had seen the video sent text messages to Mrs. Q., calling her names. The teacher asked how they found out.

On the following Monday in school, one of the friends told the principal that Mrs. Q. had had sex with Andrew. An administrator and a police officer confronted Andrew. On the way to the interview, Andrew deleted the video that he had taken of the sex act. When the officer asked him for his phone, Andrew refused at first but later complied. "I've always had problems with authority." Andrew denied that anything had happened. The school authorities called Andrew's parents and told them that he was the victim of an assault from an adult.

On mental status examination, Andrew presented as a tall, casually dressed adolescent. He had a good vocabulary and spoke openly, often with pressure of speech and anxiety. Affect varied from depression to fear, guilt and anxiety. Thinking was logical and goal-directed. There was no evidence of delusions or hallucinations. Andrew was oriented as to time person and place.

"She got out. That's why I am so scared."

Third Diagnostic Interview with Andrew

During this interview, Andrew continued to tell me about his responses to the abuse by his teacher. I asked him about the symptoms that his parents had described to me. At the end of the interview. I considered various diagnostic possibilities.

Andrew was at home making up schoolwork. He would be homeschooled for the rest of the year. He liked the isolation because Mrs. Q. could not get to him. When he went to school occasionally to meet with teachers and go over the work he has been doing, he wore a hoodie so that he would not be recognized. School officials tried to get Andrew to return to school, but he refused. Concentrating on schoolwork was very difficult due to intrusive thoughts and fears.

"My paranoia is getting worse."

Recently, when his father was walking behind him on the stairs, the clip clop of his shoes reminded Andrew of high heels. He was sure that it was Mrs. Q. sneaking up on him. Andrew also had had a vivid dream a week ago. He and a friend were in a car in a school parking lot. It was a big school and it was very bright outside. His principal and vice principal were there, talking about him. Then he was in a classroom. There were bright lights and porn was on his friend's computer. Suddenly the lights went out and the teacher disappeared. His father was hovering around and shot a gun in the dark. Then there was an open staircase and Andrew ran.

"Then we died. I don't know how."

Andrew reported other nightmares that were similar in nature: he was always in danger. There were human and animal attackers. Andrew felt trapped and usually died. Turning his thoughts to Mrs. Q., Andrew said, "Actually, she is free. The police haven't provided me any protection."

I then discussed his parents' description of the changes in him since the sexual abuse had occurred. Andrew agreed that he had lost twenty-five pounds. Since being home from school and feeling protected, Andrew's appetite had improved and he was gaining weight again. Acne had not been a problem before the sexual abuse. It became severe after the police investigated and Mrs. Q. had to stop teaching. The acne was better now. Andrew stays up until after midnight because he can go to the gym then and not run into people from school.

"I'm paranoid all the time about her coming to my house."

Andrew did acknowledge that he had a bat and a knife in his car. He also kept a machete by the desk in his room so that he can quickly get to it. Andrew feels sure that Mrs. Q. or her family will come after him and kill his family. Lately, Andrew's dad has been sleeping with him because Andrew yells in his sleep.

"Whenever he's away, I feel a little abandoned."

Recently, when Andrew went to his friend's house, a boy whom he didn't know asked him if it was true about Mrs. Q. Andrew got so angry that he had to be restrained. He feels safe at his friend's house because they have four pit bulls. "The four dogs made me feel real safe." Andrew and his friend spend five nights a week at each other's homes.

Andrew acknowledged that he gets angry at his mother. He doesn't know why.

Thoughts about Mrs. Q. do not intrude into his masturbation. Andrew is not talking to any girls. What happened with Mrs. Q. would come up and he would be embarrassed.

I asked Andrew about suicidal thoughts. He did have a plan to shoot himself but never actualized that or any other plan.

Psychological Testing

At my request, an experienced forensic psychologist administered a battery of psychological tests to Andrew. The following tests were administered: Shipley-2, Mini-Mental State Examination, 2nd Edition, Standard Version; Symptom Checklist for Children; Beck Depression Inventory, 2nd Edition: Conduct Disorder Scale, Personality Assessment Inventory—Adolescent and Million Clinical Multiaxial Inventory. In addition, Andrew's parents completed a background history questionnaire regarding their son. A summary of psychologist's findings and impressions follow.

On the Adverse Childhood Experiences Scale, "Andrew achieved a score of one, indicating an absence of childhood abuse, neglect, or exposure to family violence or instability." His only reported ACE involves being sexually assaulted by Ms. Q. "Cognitive tests did not indicate any clear evidence of cognitive impairment."

On the BDI-II, a self-report measure of symptoms of depression, Andrew scored in the severe range.

On the TSCC, a self-report measure of post-traumatic distress and related psychological symptoms, Andrew reported having clinically significant symptoms related to post-traumatic stress and anxiety, as well as some symptoms of depression. "He reports having numerous intrusive symptoms of post-traumatic stress, as well as the symptoms of anxious hyperarousal. He relies on dissociative defenses, including reduced response to the external environment, emotional detachment and a tendency to avoid negative emotions, as a way of avoiding intrusive thoughts and feelings. In addition, he reports having significant distress and conflict in association with sexual thoughts and experience. This is typical of sexual abuse victims."

The PAI-A is a self-report, objective measure of psychopathology and personality functioning and adolescents. "Andrew's responses to the PAI-I indicate that he is currently experiencing significant emotional distress with severe impairment in his psychosocial functioning. His self-esteem is low and he perceives himself as being powerless to change the direction of his life. He is tense and pessimistic about his future. The combination of hopelessness, agitation, confusion, and stress apparent in his responses may put him at increased risk of self harm."

On the same test, "Andrew reports having clinically significant symptoms related to anxiety, depression, and post-traumatic stress. His reported level of anxiety is high even in relation to clinical samples. His level of tension is so great that he is likely to easily feel overwhelmed so that even relatively mild stresses may precipitate a crisis in his life. While he believes he is in control of his angry feelings, he is prone to verbal outbursts, which can be intimidating to others."

On the MACI, another self-report measure of personality function and psychiatric symptoms in adolescents, "his response style indicates that he is currently experiencing feelings of extreme vulnerability associated with the current episode of turmoil." Andrew reports having recurrent problems with drinking and drug use. "He also reports the presence of clinically significant depressive symptoms, although he mostly experiences his depression as a sense of being fatigued and wanting to sleep. He is also quite negative, pessimistic, and fatalistic about his life, tending to expect the worst to happen. Socially awkward and introverted, he struggles with feelings of worthlessness and guilt. He is particularly sensitive to public humiliation and rejection."

Summary: "Andrew's test results are valid, and support diagnostic impressions related to depression, anxiety and post-traumatic stress. There is also evidence of a mild cannabis use disorder, and probably an alcohol use disorder. There is no evidence of antisocial narcissistic personality traits."

Various records were reviewed. Andrew was seen by his primary care physician several times after the sexual abuse became public. "His depression has been worsening over the last few weeks with bouts of anxiety." On another visit, he was noted to be depressed, having bad insomnia and staying in bed. Concentration was difficult. Described as a victim of molestation by his high school teacher, Andrew was experiencing death threats and was fearful of his teacher's family. Diagnoses of major depressive disorder, post-traumatic stress disorder, anxiety disorder, and acne were made.

A headline in the local newspaper read, "Teacher Suspected of Having Sexual Relations With Student, Enters Not Guilty Pleas." Law enforcement authorities were quoted as follows: "As the relationship grew, the minor and the teacher engaged in oral sex and ultimately sexual intercourse." The article included Mrs. Q.'s age and her picture. She was booked and released on bail.

Diagnosis

Using DSM-5, I made diagnoses of post-traumatic stress disorder, 309.81, and major depressive disorder, 296.22. Both diagnoses are supported by the results of psychological testing.

Treatment

Andrew was referred to a child analyst. He remained in therapy, one to two times per week, until he left for college last fall. The analyst describes some improvement in both the major depressive disorder and post-traumatic stress disorder but continuing preoccupation with concerns about attacks from the perpetrator, major social withdrawal, and interference with separation-individuation and plans for college. His extensive summary of the treatment, worthy of a paper in its own right, is included, in full, as an addendum to this paper (see below).

An additional course of individual psychotherapy, one to two times per week, for one to two years, is indicated at some point when Andrew is in his twenties. He may well need additional courses of therapy to diminish the effects of the adolescent abuse as he moves through young adulthood and into midlife. Antidepressant medication may or may not be indicated at that time.

Prognosis

If the course of therapy prescribed above is followed, the prognosis is fair to good. Andrew has been severely traumatized by his involvement with Mrs. Q., and the effects will be ongoing for many years.

Summary

This case is a perfect example of how many adolescent boys and young men's fantasies of sexual involvement with a teacher can turn into a nightmare. Andrew was aggressively pursued by Mrs. Q. Despite considerable ambivalence about her advances, he clearly experienced excitement and pleasure and bragged to his friends. However, it is also clear that he made no efforts to initiate sexual involvement on his own, and indeed, tried to maintain a distance from his teacher, something that over the course of two school years, she refused to allow. Following the discovery of the sexual involvement by school officials, police, family, and peers, Andrew's social and adolescent sexual development came to a halt. He remained profoundly traumatized by the sexual interaction and its consequences, was suffering from two severe psychiatric diagnoses, was withdrawn socially and emotionally and had an uncertain late adolescent and young adult future.

ELIJAH

The evaluation consisted of one diagnostic interview with mother and two with Elijah. In addition, psychological testing was administered and various records were reviewed.

Diagnostic Interview with Mother On the Telephone

Due to a disability, mother was unable to attend in person and was interviewed on the telephone. The absence of a doctor/patient relationship and confidentiality were explained. Elijah was sixteen at the time of the evaluation.

Mother provided identifying information, an account of the sexual abuse, a description of symptoms and a developmental history. Elijah's family consisted of the following individuals: father and mother, both in their thirties. Mother—age thirty-four, was disabled. The parents were never married. Mother lived with father for twenty years until recently. Father was in Elijah's life from birth until age fifteen. The boy sees his father every three to four months. Elijah has several siblings. The family was living in housing provided by a social service agency.

Mother provided the following information about the sexual abuse. The perpetrator was a female teacher in her forties. She taught junior high school and was an advisor to both boys and girls. Mother knew Ms. W.: she often helped the family out by driving the children to and from school.

Several months before the evaluation, one of Elijah's siblings called mother and said that Elijah didn't meet his friends as expected. When mother came home one day, Ms. W. and her live-in boyfriend were there. They explained that Elijah was at Ms. W.'s house because when Ms. W.'s boyfriend had come home earlier that day, he found Elijah there. Elijah immediately jumped the back fence and ran. When caught, he said he was just visiting. Ms. W. was in her bathrobe. Her boyfriend told mother that he thought Elijah and Ms. W. were sexually involved. Mother told him he was crazy and asked the man to leave. Ms. W. denied any involvement with Elijah.

A few days later, mother discovered messages between Ms. W. and Elijah on his Facebook page. They were explicitly sexual. Mother sought the advice of a family member who advised her to go to the police. Mother gave the authorities the phone that contained the explicit sexual messages.

When confronted by officers, Elijah at first denied, but later admitted, to the sexual involvement. He had detailed information about Ms. W.'s body and her bedroom. The teacher was arrested and bail was set. Elijah told his mother that they had had oral and anal sex, and intercourse, approximately thirty times. Ms. W. had an advisory period early in the day and Elijah had a class at that time. He was absent for more than fifty days from that class. Overall, Elijah missed more than one hundred days of school.

The relationship started approximately a year ago. Elijah had found Ms. W. crying one day in her classroom. She explained that she had had a fight with her boyfriend. When Elijah kissed her, Ms. W. returned the kiss. The sexual relationship that evolved over time took place in the classroom and in Ms. W.'s house and car. Elijah was a virgin before his relationship with Ms.

W. The teenager was taken for a rape protocol interview. He did not want a woman interviewer. Mother sought therapy funds from victim of crime and Elijah began to see a counselor. I asked mother to tell me how the sexual relationship with Ms. W. had affected Elijah and the family.

"He's very closed."
"He doesn't go out as much as he used to." Elijah stays in the house and plays video games.
"Hard time to get him to go back to school." Elijah and his siblings transferred to another high school.
"He didn't want anyone to know."

Because he was embarrassed, Elijah told everyone in school that one of his friends was involved with Ms. W., not he.

"He doesn't sleep well."
"He feels guilty. It's his fault."
"He says he loves her."
"He's not the same kid I raised."
"He still wants to be with her."

Elijah tells his older brother that when he is eighteen, mother will not be able to stop him from being with Ms. W.

Elijah became very upset recently when he saw Ms. W. at a gas station. She tried to talk with him.

"He is depressed. He says he feels so down."
"He feels it's his fault—what happened to the teacher."
"I can't get him to realize it's not his fault."

Elijah did not have any prior emotional problem. "He was a happy teenager. Always playing basketball. He loved basketball."

Developmental History

The following developmental history was provided by mother. Elijah was bottle fed for two years. Developmental milestones were several months late. Mother was the primary caretaker. Father was sporadically involved. Elijah was toilet trained by age three.

In elementary school, Elijah was an average student. He was quiet, had a lot of friends, and was well-behaved. The family had very meager financial resources. As elementary school progressed, Elijah became very interested in sports and participated on school and neighborhood teams.

Puberty occurred at thirteen. During middle and high school, Elijah needed extra help with reading and writing but was a standout athletically, lettering in multiple sports. He had not had any problems with the police, drugs, or alcohol when he became involved with Ms. W.

First Diagnostic Interview with Elijah

Elijah presented as a muscular, bearded teenager who looked much older than his sixteen years. He was shy but cooperative. Elijah was focused on improving his grades so he could continue to play on the school's basketball team. He loved sports and art because "it gets my mind off stuff."

When I asked about his family Elijah said that his "original dad left a while ago." He lived with his mother and siblings in an apartment that was provided for them.

"We 'make the best of it.'"

When I inquired about his friends, Elijah said, "I don't try to keep friends anymore. I want to be by myself." After his relationship with Ms. W. was revealed, some of his friends called him weird, others were angry because she had to leave, and some thought he was a stud. Elijah did not tell anyone while the affair was going on. When I asked why, he replied, "No one else's business."

"She made me the happiest person ever. She took him places and bought food. She would just take care of me." They liked to eat out and went to one movie. Elijah did not know whether Ms. W. was ever married. Other teachers didn't know what was happening.

When I asked how he felt when the relationship ended, Elijah replied, "She cared about me and I care about her. We both said that we loved each other. I always want to see her again." He didn't know what had happened to her.

On mental status examination, Elijah presented as a stocky, well-built adolescent. He appeared to weigh over 200 pounds. The teenager had a good vocabulary and had no difficulty expressing his thoughts. He described himself as "Lonely. I feel no one understands. I really loved her. She loved me too, but they don't understand because she is so much older." Affect varied from bland to sad. Thinking was logical and goal-directed. Elijah was oriented as to time, person and place and interpreted proverbs abstractly.

"I just miss her. I think about her every day." His mother has been "comforting."

It was the principal's idea for him to change schools after the affair became public. Elijah talked to the school police and then a detective. At first, he denied the relationship. The detective found messages on his Facebook page. Elijah was interviewed at a hospital by a man.

Elijah had his first sexual experience with Ms. W. He had never had a girlfriend or kissed a girl before. Their first kiss took place in the classroom.

Elijah kissed her first. She told him that he didn't treat her like her boyfriend did. Elijah had seen some X-rated movies on the Internet. A week later, they kissed again in the classroom. At the third meeting in her car, approximately a week later; Ms. W. touched Elijah's penis in his pants, and he touched her breasts.

During their fourth encounter, they had intercourse in the classroom. Both were naked. The doors were locked and the blinds closed. The sex took place on the floor on a blanket and lasted approximately fifteen minutes. Elijah did not use a condom, and he ejaculated inside of her. Ms. W. said that she had an IUD. After they finished both said it felt great.

Second Diagnostic Interview with Elijah

A few days before the second interview, Elijah saw Ms. W. while he was walking to the school bus. He became very upset and wondered how long she had been out of jail. Why hadn't she tried to contact him? They had not seen each other for several months. Elijah began to cry because he was glad to see her. She looked at him but didn't speak.

They had sex approximately thirty times. Ms. W. suggested oral sex. It was great and "would lead to other sex." Elijah would ejaculate in her mouth. Performing oral sex on her "seemed natural." They had sex at school seventeen times, in her car five times and intercourse at her house approximately seven or eight times.

After her boyfriend would leave for work, Ms. W. would call Elijah. She was free first period, and he missed class. After having sex, they would drive to school together. Anal sex occurred twice. Condoms were not used and pregnancy was never talked about. Elijah has not had sex since their relationship. He thinks of Ms. W. when he masturbates.

In regard to the effects on him as a result of the discovery of the relationship, Elijah agreed with his mother that he was very closed. "I don't like being involved with other people. I don't want them to find out." When I asked if he was ashamed, Elijah replied that he was "of people making fun of me. Not of the sex."

Elijah stays at home because he doesn't want anyone to see him. People made fun of him "a lot." "People still talk about it on Facebook." Maybe eighty people made fun of him. Elijah was very happy that the principal suggested a change of school.

He agreed that he was not sleeping well because of all "the dreams I have about her." Elijah dreams about Ms. W. approximately three times a week. These dreams wake him up and "I don't go back to sleep. I just can't. The dreams are of having sex with her." In the dreams, both say that they love each other. It's a happy dream until he wakes up.

Elijah feels guilty because "if I had deleted the text messages, she wouldn't have gotten into trouble." He agreed with his mother that he had become more secretive. He also agrees that he is depressed—"Being sad about not being able to go out of the house." Elijah does have thoughts of hurting himself because "Things would be better if I were dead." These thoughts occur once in a while but have not led to any actions.

Elijah tries to work out at a gym to take his mind off of what happened. He is not teased there because no one knows what happened. His family is in a tough spot. "It's hard. My mother struggles to pay the bills. We always have food but we're barely making it." They live in one room. Elijah had just begun therapy. He liked it.

Psychological Testing

The psychologist administered a full battery of psychological tests and conducted a clinical interview. Relevant findings and comments are summarized here.

Traumatic Symptom Checklist for Children: "It may be inferred that Elijah was indeed exposed to a traumatic sexual experience, which in turn has led to a number of defensive maneuvers in order to deal with the negative affects associated with such experiences." The post-traumatic stress scale was elevated. The test indicates that Elijah is responding to a traumatic experience that seems to be clearly related to sexual behaviors.

A similar result with regard to the presence of traumatic stress was noted in the PAI-A. The presence of physiological effects of depression highlight Elijah's lack of psychological mindedness. Emotions tend to manifest themselves in somatic terms. Mental confusion as well as the experience of self doubt and lower self confidence also appeared to be highlighted by the PAI-A profile.

Summary: the overall assessment and findings from the present evaluation suggest that Elijah is experiencing much greater internal difficulties, confusion and distress than his overt symptomatology may suggest. This distress appears to be related, at least in part, to a distinct traumatic experience associated with sexuality, one to which Elijah is trying to adapt to as best he possibly can, based on his overall described cognitive and personality style.

Review of Records

The complaint against the school district was for negligence, negligent supervision, negligent hiring and retention, negligent failure to warn, train or educate; intentional infliction of emotional distress and sexual harassment. "For eight months, W., Elijah's teacher; repeatedly engaged in illegal sex on and off campus. Sexual acts included intercourse, oral sex, touching, contact with each other's buttocks, breasts, genitals, and verbal sexual communications."

Facebook messages described explicit sexual comments and statements of mutual love between Elijah and Ms. W., and school records confirmed a large number of absences throughout the school year.

Diagnosis

Using DSM-5, I made the following diagnoses:

Sexual abuse of a child, confirmed, initial encounter, 995.54.
Victim of crime, 62.89
Post-traumatic stress disorder with depression, 309.81

Treatment

Individual psychotherapy, two times per week, for two to three years, conducted by a child or adolescent psychiatrist or psychologist with extensive experience in treating sexual abuse victims was recommended. At some point when Elijah is in his twenties, a second course of individual psychotherapy two times a week, for one to two years, is indicated. Antidepressant medication may be useful during the course of either or both psychotherapies. The goal of treatment is to diminish the effect of the trauma on Elijah's late adolescent and young adult development. No matter how successful the therapeutic efforts may be, there will be negative effects on future development throughout adulthood.

Prognosis

If the course of treatment outlined above is followed, the prognosis for diminishing the effects of the sexual abuse is fair to good.

Summary

The prolonged sexual abuse has had a profound negative effect on this young man's self-esteem and adolescent development. A virgin at the time, he has his first sexual experience with an adult woman rather than with a chronological peer. Instead of experiencing a number of adolescent infatuation's, which allow those in their teens to slowly integrate their sexually mature bodies within carrying relationships, Elijah's first sexual experience was with an adult woman who was an authority figure. At present, his continuing feelings of passion and love for Ms. W. dominate his intrapsychic world. In addition, public knowledge of the sexual relationship has seriously undermined peer relationships and self-esteem and has resulted in the necessity of changing schools.

DISCUSSION

The following discussion is intended to compare and contrast the experience of these three boys and understand their sexual abuse in the context of psychoanalytic developmental theory.

Age of the sexual abuse: Jack was thirteen when he was abused. Elijah and Andrew were fifteen. Jack and Elijah were virgins. All three of the boys, who were in early and middle adolescence, looked much older than their chronological ages.

The perpetrators: In each instance, the perpetrator appeared to be searching for young, vulnerable, sexually mature boys. The facts that are known about them are interesting. Two of the women were in their forties, the third in her thirties. Two were married and had children of approximately the same age as their victims. The third was in a long-term relationship. Thoughts about their motivation are speculative, but we can safely say that they were all dealing with universal, midlife issues about aging and sexual attractiveness and were making the inevitable midlife questioning about choices made, such as husband and children, and alternative paths not taken (Colarusso, 1992). All perpetrators lost their jobs and were brought before the court. Two served time in jail, and the third was placed on probation. All three are registered sex offenders—a stigma that will be with them for the rest of their lives. I have no information about whether any of them engaged in any form of treatment.

Grooming: In somewhat different ways, each of the perpetrators groomed their victims. Mrs. L. began grooming Jack by talking about wanting to divorce her husband. As they parted the first time, she pulled his face into her breasts. Further, Mrs. L. responded quickly to Jack's request for alcohol and the use of her car in exchange for sex. She also gave him money. Jack was curious about sex and drinking and readily responded to Mrs. L.'s advances.

Mrs. Q, on the other hand, spent months pursuing Andrew. She went to his sporting events, formed a casual relationship with his mother, and told him that because he was so tall and mature, he was special. Rules didn't apply to him. She sent him nude photos of herself and when he seemed to be hesitant, got in his car and performed oral sex. His ambivalence was exemplified by the fact that he did not get a full erection or ejaculate. After Andrew withdrew from her for months after the fellatio, Mrs. Q. again went on the attack and that time, succeeded in seducing Andrew. They had intercourse at her home on a kitchen counter. Her persistence and his curiosity and desire to brag to his buddies resulted in his compliance and started the chain of disastrous consequences that followed.

Ms. W. insinuated herself into Elijah's life, befriending the family and driving the children to school. She was aware of the absence of a father and the extreme financial difficulty that the family was enduring. Of the three boys, Elijah was the most vulnerable. Although clearly curious sexually, he had greater needs for love, money, and security. Unlike the other two boys, Elijah was "in love" with Ms. W. and was planning to marry her when he was eighteen years old, emotionally disregarding her unavailability. This was not the normal developmental early and mid-adolescent infatuation that we see directed toward teachers, rock stars, and other fantasied objects. That infatuation furthers emotional and sexual separation from the infantile objects by providing a safe object on which to project masturbatory fantasies. This "love" was an attempt to fill a deep emotional void.

Although economic deprivation and emotional vulnerability clearly played a significant role in why Jack and Elijah were so vulnerable to their perpetrators, an even more powerful vulnerability in all three boys resulted from the destabilizing effect of testosterone on the latency and early adolescent ego and superego. As described by Blos (1967), the imbalance between drive and structure that is so characteristic of adolescence was very prominent and instrumental in the boys' responses.

In the 1980s, Cath, Ross, and Gurwitt (1982, 1989) made major advances in the psychoanalytic understanding of the role of fathers in the development of their children. Their pioneering work served as a theoretical background for my comments on the roles that the boys' fathers played in their sons' development and response to the perpetrators. Jack and Elijah were not raised by their fathers. They won their Oedipal victories without a fight. Jack openly talked about wanting to be the man of the house, until he was faced with the burden of actually being a husband and father with a child at age eighteen. He verbalized several times how much he wished his father had been there to teach him how to be a man. He and Elijah did not have a male progenitor to teach them about sexuality and to set limits on unsafe sexual and illegal behavior.

Andrew did have a very involved father in his life. That explains, in part, Andrew's ambivalence about Mrs. Q.'s advances. After the abuse became public, when father was at home, Andrew felt protected; even to the point of having father sleep in the same bed with him. But when father was away, powerful Oedipally based, sexual feelings toward mother—undoubtedly stimulated by the sexual experiences with Mrs. Q.—emerged. The power of these impulses was so strong that they were defended against by verbal rages at mother and on occasion actually pushing her. This behavior maintained an emotional distance from mother while at the same time expressing his sexual conflict by accusing her of cheating on her husband.

Effects on adolescent development in each of the boys: According to his mother, Jack wanted to be the man of the house. Having intercourse at age thirteen falsely boosted his sense of masculinity and intensified his Oedipal victory. Without paternal influence and limit setting, he became a father at seventeen. By eighteen, he developed strong feelings of shame and disgust, as did the other boys. Jack and Elijah talked of losing respect for women. The sexual abuse undermined the early adolescent development task of becoming comfortable with the body as a sexual instrument and the mid-adolescent developmental task of gradual sexual involvement with peers.

At 18, Jack described being the man of the house as a huge burden, not something to be desired. Jack wished he had known his father, "to learn about becoming a man. He never accepted me." In addition to developing a drinking problem that he was attempting to control, Jack embarrassed his family and was teased by his peers for having sex with an old woman "who wasn't hot."

Thrust into parenthood before he was ready financially, educationally, or emotionally, and without a securely committed relationship with his child's mother, Jack's late adolescent and young adulthood will be equally compromised. Instead of the late adolescent years being available for increasing autonomy and a wide variety of educational, life, and sexual experiences, thus facilitating the path to a productive, stable young adulthood; Jack's hope is to finish high school, work in construction, and buy a house—if he and his child's mother are still together. Hopefully, he will integrate a sustained paternal identity and responsibility and continue to think of his child as "happiness." Both he and the child are at considerable risk developmentally for the foreseeable future.

All three of these cases are examples of what I presented in my 2010 book, *The Long Shadow of Sexual Abuse: Developmental Effects Across the Life Cycle* (2010), namely that the effects of childhood and adolescent sexual abuse are ongoing and life-long and affect not only the victims, but family members as well.

At first, Andrew boasted to his friends about his "conquest" but his feelings rapidly changed to embarrassment after word of his sexual involvement with Mrs. Q. spread. The embarrassment was quickly followed by a full-blown symptomatic response that included nightmares, panic attacks, and fears of being killed by Mrs. Q. and her family. Andrew lost twenty-five pounds and developed acne. He became fearful of going out in public, altered his appearance, and withdrew from school. An exceptional student who was headed for college, Andrew no longer felt that he could feel safe away from home.

According to both of his parents, and his own account, Andrew became severely regressed. His parents described him as childlike, and he said, "I know I look like a man but I'm a boy." Although there was some reality to

Andrew's concerns for his safety—tampons were left on the hood of his car, the family home was papered, and friends told him that Mrs. Q.'s family was coming after him—he became openly paranoid, repeatedly seeing Mrs. Q. outside his home or following him in his car when no one was there.

Elijah retreated into himself and his home. He stopped talking, changed schools, and lost interest in learning. Like the other two boys, he experienced great social embarrassment when the sexual relationship became public, in sharp contrast to the boasting and bragging that was present earlier.

Unlike Andrew and Jack, Elijah remains deeply infatuated with Ms. W. He wants to marry her when he turns eighteen. Elijah was raised by his mother. His father was only sporadically involved in his life. He managed to follow the rules and control his behavior during latency without paternal guidance; but once the hormonal upsurge of puberty occurred, shattering whatever intra-psychic stability that had been achieved during latency, Elijah became sexually curious, and because of his emotional neediness, highly susceptible to sexual abuse. Like the other two boys, and almost all sexual abuse victims, Elijah blamed himself for what happened. He felt guilt for what he thinks he did to Ms. W.

Other effects: Because the sexual abuse occurred in early adolescence, Jack and Elijah were not able to, as many boys do, use their female teachers as safe masturbatory objects in the service of the early adolescent tasks of integrating sexual arousal with fantasied objects and separating them from incestuous objects—both being essential parts of the second individuation. (Blos, 1967).

Andrew's abuse occurred in mid-adolescence. He had made significant progress toward integrating the early adolescent developmental tasks just described and had had sexual experience with age appropriate peers; but the integration of a comfortable, modulated, controlled sexual behavior was far from complete when the process was derailed by the sexual abuse.

Therapy: Jack saw a social worker for eighteen months on a weekly basis. He said it helped. Elijah has not had any therapy. When I approached the subject, he resisted, saying that he didn't want to do anything that would question his love for Ms. W and her supposed love for him.

The future: Within a few years, all three adolescents will enter young adulthood. Because of the emotional wreckage that took place in adolescence as a result of the sexual abuse by their teachers, they will be unprepared to address and master the developmental tasks of young adulthood such as the third individuation (Mahler et al., 1975), the development of the capacity for intimacy and preparing to work; to name just a few.

As described by Mahler and her colleagues (Mahler et. al., 1975), the separation-individuation process in infancy is responsible for the establishment of a stable sense of self and the capacity to relate to others. Building on Mahler's work, Blos, senior (Colarusso, 1979), described the process of psychological separation from parents in adolescence as the second individuation. Continuing their work into young adulthood, I (1990) described the third individuation as "that continuous process of elaboration of self and differentiation from objects that occurs in the developmental phases of young and middle adulthood" (p.135).

At eighteen, Jack is ill-prepared to support a wife and child. Andrew does not feel he can leave home to go to college. Elijah is infatuated with his perpetrator instead of moving toward emotional autonomy from his mother. None of the three are gradually progressing toward a comfortable sense of separation from parents and the establishment of a sense of autonomy and independence that is at the core of the third individuation.

All three now have considerable sexual experience, so in a sense they have mastered the adolescent task of becoming comfortable with the body as a sexual instrument; but none are well-equipped to engage the late adolescent/young adult task of developing the capacity for intimacy. Erickson (1963) defined the major developmental dichotomy of his Stage VI, young adulthood, as intimacy versus stagnation. Intimacy required one to "experience someone else's needs and concerns as equally important as one's own" (p. 31). The capacity for intimacy has roots in the quality of the early parent-child relationships, the successful resolution of the Oedipal conflict, and adolescent sexual experimentation. As defined by Nemiroff and myself (Colarusso and Nemiroff, 1981), adult intimacy presupposes a significant relationship with a partner that is elaborated over time and usually is associated with deep emotional commitment and shared parenthood.

As they progress into young adulthood, these young men will have much to overcome if they are to achieve intimacy. Because of the sexual abuse, all three victims distrust women. All three feel used and abused by their perpetrators. Andrew and Elijah do not have age-appropriate relationships with the opposite sex. Jack has a girlfriend and a child. He and his girlfriend, who live with his mother, "may" buy a house if they are still together in the future. Their relationship began during a drunken sexual encounter that led to a pregnancy and an impulsive decision to marry—hardly an intimate experience. Their child is clearly at risk emotionally and developmentally.

All three are struggling with the adolescent/young adult developmental task of preparing to obtain further education or training that would allow them to support themselves and their families in adulthood. At 18, Jack already has a girlfriend and a child and no concrete means of supporting them. Andrew did not feel that he could leave home to go to college, but with the help of extended psychotherapy with a child analyst, he did. Instead of focusing on formal learning, Elijah pines for his perpetrator.

So, I hope I've convinced the men and the women in the audience that sex between female teachers and male students, or between any adult woman and their son's teenage friends, is not a good idea. But from the twinkle in the eyes of just a few of you, and you know who you are, maybe I haven't convinced everyone.

ADDENDUM BY GORDON CARAS, PHD

"John Doe" is nineteen-year-old male who suffered from post-traumatic stress disorder subsequent to being sexually and emotionally abused by his female teacher, a woman in her forties. The first incident occurred three months into his sophomore year when she gave him fellatio. A year later, she engaged him to perform coitus with her. Throughout this period, she intermittently threatened to kill him or herself if he disclosed these events to anyone. School officials learned about the transgression shortly after the second incident and reported it to the police. She was convicted and sentenced approximately eight months later.

John was an attractive, athletic adolescent who for years had felt alienated from his peers. A second-generation immigrant, he had lived in multiple locations up through his eighth grade academic year. Consequently, he kept changing schools every few years. This totaled to five different schools, which, in combination with being homeschooled at different times between two countries, resulted in John being alienated from his peers. No sooner would he begin to develop friendships that he relocated, challenged thereby to develop new ones. His father's work demands required multiple relocations between the United States and another country.

In ninth grade, John finally had a solid group of friends that he expected would remain so throughout his high school years. No more family relocations were on the horizon. His involvement with his high school peers and his team buddies promoted his independence and separation from his family. Just a year earlier, John was homeschooled in an environment that is best characterized a caricature of a spirited and highly enmeshed Mediterranean system.

In his sophomore year, John was enrolled in the perpetrator's class. She singled him out. Initially she texted him when he missed class to inquire about his status and express concern for his well-being. Over time, he realized that she was flirting with him and transgressing the teacher-student divide. Though initially subtle, her advances became more overt, more extreme. She eventually sent him provocative texts, some including nude pictures of herself. She asked him to send him pictures of his penis. Ambivalently, he complied.

By then, there was no ambiguity whether it was merely his imagination, excited by his hormones, which impregnated his perception that she was sexually seducing him. It was indisputable. Earlier on, he had intuitively sensed that she was seducing him in the first month of class. But it all seemed too surreal, too weird, for, he shared, she was approximately his mother's age, and more, he didn't find her attractive.

Three months into his sophomore year, she gave him fellatio for forty-five minutes; he did not, or could not, reach organism. He felt too estranged from himself in what he characterized as a dreamlike event. It seems he escaped in his mind without being physically departing. Not until a year later did he realize that had felt throughout the preceding months estranged from himself, withdrawn, inwardly numb, and operating as a "false-self." These descriptive and dynamic features, along with other he described, indicated that he dealt with the trauma by depersonalizing and significantly compartmentalizing his feelings, which is a form of a dissociative disorder, secondary to his PTSD.

For months afterward, she threatened kill him or herself if he told anyone. Immediately after the incident, John demonstrated clinical (PTSD) features, their scope and severity increasing over many months. For example, he was terrified and felt estranged from himself and others. His appearance and functioning deteriorated. He withdrew from his family, lost twenty-five pounds, acne emerged all over his face, he carried an knife in his car and a machete in his bedroom, encouraged his father to buy a gun, and more. He felt his teacher was casing his house. And he was terrified, therefore, to leave his house and resisted sleeping due to nightmares occurring of her killing him. (Since the clinical manifestations were specified in detail on a psychiatric evaluation, I won't discuss them.)

The second sexual violation occurred approximately a year after the first. For about six months prior, and over the summer between school years, he heard from her less frequently and was hoping the ordeal was over; she had stopped texting, threatening, and soliciting him, and he avoided her. But shortly into his junior year, it picked up again, once they had contact through school-related activities. Eventually she instigated a second sexual transgression at her home. Both intoxicated, they had coitus. Rumors spread, and within the first week the principal, John's family, and the police were notified.

Treatment and Concurrent Formulations

John began his intensive, twice a week, psychodynamic psychotherapy five months following the second sexual transgression by his teacher. The immediate goal was to help him mange his debilitating, acute symptoms that impaired his routine functioning in multiple domains, such as maintaining his academic studies, sleep cycles, and more. The longer term therapeutic aspiration has been for him to gain some notion, if not some limited insight, into how he organizes his experiences with himself and others in defensive ways that in turn virtually are a repeat of the original trauma on an interpersonal level, and felt as such to varying shades of intensity. Any access to these more opaque defensive and dynamically unconscious activities would emerge in his relationship with me and be interpretable to varying degrees over time.

Initially John was guarded, self-admittedly oppositional, and mistrusting. He had shared up front that he despised authority figures—principals, police officers, and so forth. He felt they all abuse their power and ride high on their own egos just for the sake of it. An added challenge was that John was an adolescent. Hence, he was normatively striving for independence and autonomy contrary to developing a dependency or involvement with me, yet another adult figure.

The first eight months of John's therapy were unsteady and rocky. His moods and thought processes dramatically fluctuated. Within the same session, he would swing from being emotionally present, focused and engaging to being quite detached, dissociated, suspicious, and depressed. His sleep patterns and motivation for help were no less erratic. He periodically missed sessions for having confused the days of the week or sessions times. We consistently made them up, however; and in doing so, he discovered me more flexible and accommodating than he had anticipated. I disconfirmed his pathogenic beliefs and this slowly made way for new experiences to emerge. As well, I occasionally caught hold of his periodic transference innuendos and, openly and measuredly, affirmed their relevance, always empathically, and always in the neighborhood of immediate, tangible experience that we could examine together. Here I was demonstrating that the soil he and I were cultivating would not impede his independence and autonomy. However, given his nature and age, he was restless; his adolescent thrust for freedom and autonomy, strong, and this in turn was a strong head wind opposing the therapy.

Nonetheless, I continued to incrementally disconfirm his preemptive belief that I was not truly trustable, if not adversary or one who sought to impede his independence or fault him for it. We continued to join in different ways, sometimes by discussing existentially related books or poetry we were mutually familiar with. He enjoyed and prided his skill in interpreting different creative works, an activity I analogized to what he and I were doing, now he himself and his inner life, the living work at hand. He responded well to this extension by opening up more about himself. This opened a door for us to begin to explore the reasons why he felt those in power let him down in regard to his teacher violating him sexually.

As we walked along beyond that door, I watched closely how he was experiencing yet another essential stranger probing into his personal boundaries. Would he experience me as wolf in sheep's clothing, surreptitiously using the process of therapy itself in the pretense to help him but in fact gaming to hurt him? Would he dynamically configure and feel it as a repetition of his molestation? And if so, to what degree would I be able to use the transference as a mutative aid to illuminate with him his inner life, dynamically and structurally taken? This, unfortunately, is typically unreachable in a twice a week therapy, which, although one may aspire for in depth access and structural reworking, often settles for symptom abatement.

Yet, my knowing this mutative power differential between what a full analysis offers from a twice a week psychotherapy was an ever-present dimension in the process. It was critical, therefore, that the therapeutic grasps not zealously exceed what's reachable; otherwise, blind enactments would likely materialize and interpretable projection identifications find vigor and life to pervert the therapeutic process. And more, it would risk repeating in symbolic form derivatives of his molestation, rejoined by an intrusion of my countertransference, by a failure of limits being imposed on the spontaneous actives of yet another adult.

John eventually settled "some" into his therapy beyond the initial phase. However, throughout, the quality of his commitment unvaryingly shifted like an ocean tide, as did the force of his presence like a waxing and waning moon. For stretches of time, he was invested in the therapy by all measures: he was on time; motivated to feel relief from his suffering; spoke about his issues; opened up new emotional avenues to explore; and commented on the process. Then, suddenly, it changed: he missed sessions; proved unmotivated and worried he might lose his creative edge if he felt better; attacked implicitly and devalued explicitly the validity and efficacy of talk therapy.

When John depreciated the therapy, I empathically affirmed the merit of his feelings in light of the context of his recent history and suffering along with therapy involving a slow, often invisible process at play. I also added, interpreting upwardly, that it understandably takes time to let his guard down, to open himself up to someone new—me, a virtual stranger—and that I would be more surprised and concerned if he instead immediately trusted me fully or merely complied outwardly with the program, a mere mask of sincerity.

Clearly, my choice of terms and interpretation called up his molestation via displacement; that is, I silently took his disparaging the therapy as a displaced commentary upon the sincerity of my intentions. His devalued stance casted me as a virtual predator of sorts. It was a transference manifestation pregnant with mutative potential. But, it was too early to interpret what was compressed in his virtual attacks in depth, or downwardly. That would take time, and with that, interpretive timing, tact and dose in unison, which often is a Rubix Cube with adolescents in general.

As the months progressed, in the throes of peak moments laden with therapeutic potential, I eagerly intuited the depth and saw the horizon of insight and healing he could potentially gain over time, but probably wouldn't get there. For the treatment modality, two times per week typically does not vitalize and promote a fuller, interpretable analytic process. And he, an adolescent, ambivalent and reluctant regarding therapy and striving for independence, was certainly not going to increase the weekly session frequency. I tried some, and he denied. So I laid the groundwork for this possibility downstream while continuing to solidify a therapeutic alliance for the work at hand.

Curiously, his session frequency—an enactment may well have unfolded; in my eagerness to help him, if acted rather than mentalized and eventually used interpretatively, I instead may have brought about an unanalyzable iatrogenic outcome. And this itself would be a form of repetition of his molestation by his teacher, aborting insight into his mental affections and impulses that shape his attitude and behaviors interpersonally now and downstream.

Even now, fourteen months into the therapy, he periodically exhibited mistrust about my sincerity in helping him. However, he was now able to explore the upper strata and preconscious bases of his mistrusting feelings and attitudes and to varying degrees their deeper dynamics and structures, unlike earlier in the work. He is less suspicious, more trusting of my objectives.

With all that, John has continued to make steady gains. He graduated from high school and was accepted at a state university. His acute symptoms are now mostly a memory, and the event of their origination, too, is receding into history. What remains, however, is his deep mistrust of women. And this is the realm that, mentioned earlier, is not easily accessible unless vivified, illuminated, and interpreted in the transference. Simply, it will require more time, more weekly sessions. And it would be incompatible with his aim; his gaze is already ahead elsewhere, he, rightfully eager, is soon to launch from home onto college. What will follow him there, though, will be his preemptive mistrust and animus toward women. His contempt for them is always close at hand. Some of this, it seems, is an extension of his family dynamics, an outcome and continuity of his relationships with his mother and older sister, both of whom he finds unbearably aggressive. But certainly the consequential effects of his molestation are significant in the equation.

John upholds a high standard of loyalty and fidelity in his relationships. Also, he is extremely sensitive to how others respond to his story; his molestation. If he catches molecules of others implying he enjoyed it, he is quick to anger and has to restrain himself from losing it, which means attacking the other person verbally, wishing it were physically. No bravado spirit to found, unlike earlier in the locker room at high school.

John has dated some. He even carried a relationship through a few months with a young lady his age. He was emotionally and sexually intimate with her. But he was quick to fault her, severely and unforgivingly, when she proved inconsistent on different matters. His tolerance for ambiguity with women is exceedingly very low and by default, he reflexively rejects what is not understood in the dance of intimacy. Yet ambiguity is an essential ingredient in all relationships during all stages of life. Laying the groundwork for what lies ahead, we discussed these challenges that await him so that, when they arise, he has a GPS to resume his treatment downstream as needed. Maybe then we can dive into deeper realms once he has traversed his adolescent passage more fully, when submitting himself into an intimate relationship with another adult is not as threatening or at cross purposes with his thrust and thirst for independence and launching.

DISCUSSION

Oscar Wilde said that there are two tragedies in life: one is *not getting* what you want and the other *is getting* what you want. Whether this may capture what John experienced, and if so, in what mode and to what degree, is speculative; he did not consciously feel sexually attracted to this teacher nor organically aroused. Given his reported conscious experience, it's critical, for the purposes of psychoanalytic rigor, not to assume a prior what remains to demonstrated empirically on its own terms clinically for theoretical verification, or commit a *petitio principi*.

John didn't or couldn't reach orgasm after his teacher gave him fellatio for forty-five minutes. Nor could he get fully engorged. He claims unequivocally that he did not feel himself sexually aroused regarding her. How best, then, to organize his treatment and experiences within an psychoanalytic scheme of understanding from the ground up invoking minimal assumptions rather than the inverse—so to minimize theoretical dogmatism?

What is indisputable is that, as an adolescent, his hormones were raging from the cannons of puberty. And adolescent boys often discover themselves sexually fantasizing about older women, their teachers included. In "discovering themselves fantasizing," this indicates that it is not a proactive process that is consciously willed. Rather, the event is more an effect or result of multifaceted and interrelated influences that escape immediate volition, since they are generated biologically and stream upward into awareness through unconscious strata in virtue of the mind's relation to the body. In a similar analogy, we don't see gravity but only experience its effects that refer to a force we call gravity.

Fantasy formations stream amongst and animate various shades of conscious unconscious activities, including dynamic operations, to manage intrapsychic conflict amongst structures developed during the first separation-individuation period years earlier, in the service of adaptation. Implicit in this developmental process is that fantasy-memory-complexes develop and organize experiences throughout life. We saw some of his fantasy-memory-complexes at play in the transference manifestations with his defensive activities and me.

During adolescence, the biological engines and underpinnings storm into awareness sexual excitations unlinked from the finer tuned qualities of its manifest object. These urges run a typical course that are eventually actualized in some measure with ones cohorts on the way toward forming mature intimate relationships and adult identity consolidation. This is trend of normal sexual development.

In John's case, this common course was thwarted and perverted when his teacher molested him. A common sexually fantasy and its attendant anxieties for adolescents became a reality. It's not clear whether or to what degree John's fantasies were unconsciously operative in accordance with his sexual urges on a primordial level and thus indifferent to their object that takes form on a secondary processing, in which case lacking a representation regarding his teacher. Nonetheless, the sexual molestation was illicit, secretive, and emotionally violent. It became a living nightmare for John. He has often indicated what adversely affected him the most were her threats. He feared that she would and could kill him. The combination of the aggression in the mix of transgressing what resonates as an incest taboo was too much for John to bear. It was not surprising that, shortly after the first incident, he turned on, discolored, and denigrated his mother, his paranoid accusations about her fidelity given life in his emotional haze. He also felt most comfortable when his father was home and most protected when sleeping next to him.

John's subsequently attacking his mother and sleeping in the same room as his father may be seen as a compromise formation. John's felt his mother as a concretization and objectification of the perpetrator. His infantile repression barrier was cracked, and earlier developmental constellations, their attendant anxieties and imagined calamities, infiltrated into his contemporary experiences, less mediated due to his molestation and his regression that followed; all this, when he was already navigating tumultuous riptides and eddies inherent in adolescent regression-progression activities. At John's age, his hormones and sex drives encountered an actual transgression and thus sexual violation. His symptoms indicated that, though sexually aroused hormonally, when it became contiguous with his teacher's activities, he was understandably extremely conflicted about it. The gap was too wide in their ages, and she was the teacher.

John shared with his buddies, in a bravado spirit, the lewd pictures of herself that his teacher had sent him, as well as her texts. And expectedly, the customary culture and discourse of adolescent boys on such matters dominated the surface. Regardless, this allowed John to express his anxiety about the boundary violation in a public context. Later, he realized that he kept up the masquerade when in fact he was wishing that someone would report it on his behalf. However, invoking a bravado spirit and sharing the news also elevated John into the limelight amongst his peers as special. This must have felt good after having felt alienated from his peers for many years previously.

However, John himself didn't feel lucky. Moreover, sharing the pictures in the context of a bravado spirit may have allowed John unconsciously to displace his sexual arousal and related fantasies. It comprised a multiplicity of aims.

What otherwise animates the sublimatory effects, virtually, safely sealed from awareness in normal development; in John's case, was actualized beyond what was ordained. I suspect more damaging than the sexual transgression was the perpetrator's recurring threats to kill him. It was the worst outcome in the Oedipal constellation whose mythos merely represents the intrapsychic structural configurations that crystallize childhood development.

These structural configurations themselves reciprocally shape and color interpersonal experiences. They originally emerged from normal strife and reconciliations that incrementally appear on the plane of experience that unfolds into inner and outer fields in the formative years. These two realms—interpersonal and intrapsychic—and their interlacing were the soil of John's adolescent separation and individuation that was adversely impacted—Prometheus unbounded in the midst of the adolescent separation-individuation process. Whereas, in the first, the aim was to separate from the external parents once their internally felt presences via representations have been sufficiently developed, in the second separation, one aim is to separate from the internalized parental identifications in order to rework them to promote the consolidation of one's adult identity.

Often this is a confused and internally chaotic time for adolescents, regressions in the services of progression. In John's case, given the particular nature of his sexual traumas, what opened up for him were earlier Oedipal terrors and calamities that found anchorage in real time and flesh. Primordial states, or levels of psychic organization, intruded upon John's perceptive faculties. It was no coincidence that, within weeks after the first incident, he felt inwardly that his mother violated the family Moirai, that she transgressed the proper province comprising the family system. He accused her of having an affair. By all indices, it was unfounded. His charge bore instead the externalization and projection of his inner workings and derivatives of the sexual violation he endured secretively, a symbolic incest. And more, he only felt safe and could sleep when his father slept with him. John sought his protection not only from threats from without—the perpetrator—but also threats from within, his own unearthed Oedipal strivings that threatened to exceed its apportioned lot and reek psychic havoc. Here he also was repeating the trauma virtually, the perpetrator's seductive instigations, and what it evoked for him, but this time with his father to intervene. (A hoped for different outcome as John sought to repeat and work through the trauma.)

My hope is that John will continue to work through rather than repeat in unrecognized ways the role his fantasy-memory-complex will have upon his future relations so to convert potential repetitions into symbolic modes of expression in terms of language on his way into intimacy with others and with himself.

Chapter Five

The Seduction of Adolescent Males by Female Teachers

Why So Infrequent?

Andrew Smolar

Calvin Colarusso's chapter titled, "Be Careful What You Wish For," tells the stories of three adolescent boys who are seduced by three middle-aged women in school settings. Although Dr. Colarusso is not in the role of psychodynamic psychotherapist with any of the three boys, he does serve as their forensic consultant, and in that role, he is privy to their narratives. He also reports their mothers' accounts of their childhood developments and their observations of what happened to their sons following their sexual encounters. He also forwarded to me a description of the fourteen-month-plus therapy process conducted by Andrew's therapist, Gordon Caras, who was successful in helping Andrew process the trauma of his encounters and the post-traumatic symptomatic phase. Dr. Colarusso synthesizes the traumatic experiences of the three boys by describing the usual psychosexual developmental tasks of adolescence and how the actualization of what would ordinarily be fantasies of sexual contact with maternal substitutes is likely to be disruptive and life-altering for adolescent boys. He specifically contrasts the paths of Jack and Elijah—who are attempting to negotiate early adolescence without engaged fathers at the time of their sexual abuse—with that of Andrew. Andrew has reached mid-adolescence when recruited for sex by Mrs. Q., and he is terrified by the kindling of an Oedipal scene in which he feels enmeshed with an aggressive, sexually alive mother with whom he has transgressed.

I could speculate more about the particulars of the boys' early developments, and their vulnerability to abuse. Or I could speculate more about the psychopathology of the women who have sought out these adolescent students. Or I could add to the voluminous literature about sexual abuse, in this case discussing the less common incidence of abuse of adolescent boys by female perpetrators. I am sobered by the specter of abuse because I've seen much of it in my office and have felt the pain of patients' feelings of injustice, helplessness, fear, and self-condemnation. And almost all of the stories I've heard in torturous detail have been of adult women abused by men in childhood, resiliently finding their voices, and desperately trying not to repeat the damage with their own children.

FEMALE SEXUAL OFFENSE

I started to research the subject of female abuse of men by wondering about its incidence. Like all of you, I've heard of some of these high-profile cases—the cases of Mary Kay Letourneau and Leah Shipman are just a couple of examples. Dr. Colarusso tells us upfront that there are no references in the psychoanalytic literature to sexual abuse by adult female teachers of adolescent male students. So, I began to look for this dynamic elsewhere. I recall a movie that highlights this dynamic: *The Reader*, in which a German woman nurtures an adolescent boy and then exchanges sexual education for his reading to her. The boy is then depicted as a young adult, when he is haunted by mixed feelings of guilt, anger, and loyalty, as he remains silent about her illiteracy during her trial for war crimes; then later in his adult years when he helps her learn to read while she is imprisoned; and then in the aftermath of her suicide. I then began to scour the literature not only in our familiar psychoanalytic lexicon, but also in the trauma and criminal justice fields. Because I was curious: What dynamics underlie this kind of abuse? Are they different from what drives male abuse of women? And if male abuse of women is so much more common, why is this so?

Before examining women's sexual abuse of adolescent boys, I examined several other dyadic circumstances. Within the Catholic Church, for example, male clergy are more likely to abuse children sexually than female clergy, with the ratio at least 3:1, despite the fact that women clergy have greater exposure to children (Chibnall et al., 1998; Travers, 2006; Viano, 2007; Dura-Vila et al., 2013). Convicted pedophiles are dominantly male, comprising at least 80 percent or more of the offending population, with 80 percent of juvenile victims being female (The U.S. Department of Justice Facts and Statistics, 2018). Interestingly, in a study of sexual interest in children among an online sample of college men and women, Wurtele et al. (2013) find that 9.8 percent of men endorse at least one item associated with sexual interest in children, while 4.2 percent of women endorse the same, and a similar ratio holds for the likelihood of viewing child pornography on the internet (if individuals are assured of not being caught). Both males and females with sexual interest in children experienced higher rates of insecure parent-child attachment and childhood sexual abuse.

The literature on dating violence—which reflects responses of both perpetrators and victims—demonstrates a high incidence of female perpetration (French et al., 2014; Stemple et al., 2017; Struckman-Johnson et al., 2003), with women employing physical coercion and verbal manipulation. Dardis et al. (2013) confirm this relative symmetry between males in females in dating situations, and find that childhood experiences of maternal neglect and dating victimization predict men's sexual perpetration, while childhood sexual abuse and related negative internalizations resulting in eroded self-esteem predict women's sexual perpetration. Despite the fact that reports of maternal sexual abuse are inclined to be underreported, they have increased in the literature, and although accounts of victims reflect perhaps greater devastation, they affect far fewer victims than those injured by men (Peter, 2008). Finally, even though women's political and legal gains have resulted in their achieving greater power in the workplace, and male victims may be less likely to report harassment than women, rates of female harassment of men remain low, are largely nonsexual, more often target nonconforming gender-stereotyped males, and tend to reflect group-level dynamics rather than specific dynamics of the female-male dyad (McDonald and Charlesworth, 2015).

Female sex offenders have some characteristics in common with their male counterparts but also have important differences. Females have historically been more difficult to study for several reasons: there are fewer of them; gender stereotypes have prevented recognition of them as an authentic group (Hetherton, 1999), and this bias may interfere with the reporting of cases; and because they have been studied from prison and clinical populations as opposed men, the findings may not be applicable to the more general population (Allen, 1991; Oliver, 2007). Those limitations notwithstanding, female adolescent sex offenders are different from their male counterparts in the following ways: they typically target young children who are relatives; they often offend in the course of babysitting; they have more overt psychiatric symptoms; and their childhood households were more chaotic and abusive (greater duration and severity of sexual abuse, greater number of incestuous and total number of abusers, greater number of violent incidents within the family) than were the males' households (Bumby and Bumby, 1997; Chen and Gueta, 2016; Mathews et al., 1997, Oliver, 2007).

Adult female sex offenders have the following characteristics: they are more inclined to abuse nonrelatives; about 25 percent become involved in a teaching or mentoring relationship with a young adolescent male who becomes the victim; they tend to be confused regarding generational boundaries and demonstrate cognitive distortions in thinking of the victim as a sexually consenting adult, reflecting their denial of harmful impact to the victim; and about 25 percent are sexual predators with high additional criminality (Vandiver and Kercher, 2004; Oliver, 2007). Lower socioeconomic status, lower educational achievement, inadequate social supports, high rates of psychopathology—including ego dysfunction—and high rates of substance abuse are common within this group (DeCou et al., 2014). The literature has begun to include studies of the offense process for female offenders and how it differs from the male process (Gannon et al., 2008; Cortoni, 2015); typologies for female offenders have been developed, dividing them by age, type of victim, degree of wider criminality, and whether they include a male co-perpetrator. Rates of this latter type are approximately 20 percent, and these female offenders describe being motivated by jealousy, revenge, and/or fear vis a vis their male co-offenders (Gannon and Rose, 2008). Surveys have varied, and I recognize that some of the complexities above may prevent accurate measurements of female compared with male perpetration of sexual abuse. Still, one conclusion is incontrovertible: despite the fact that females are more often responsible for child caretaking in Western society—and thus are more exposed to children than are males—and despite the fact that girls are more often sexually abused than boys, males commit abuse at a much higher rate than females.

TESTOSTERONE—A CAUSE?

So, I wondered, could differences in testosterone levels explain the greater incidence of male abuse, given that adult males have ten times the level of total testosterone as females? The literature about testosterone and aggression is equivocal: although a few studies demonstrate that male aggression correlates with higher levels of testosterone—and even these do not establish a cause-and-effect relationship between testosterone and violent behavior—most indicate that testosterone levels correlate with transient feeling states such as arousal, dominance, and competitiveness (Bancroft, 2012). When looking closely, however, more of the evidence points to greater dominance resulting in higher testosterone levels, rather than the opposite cause and effect (Hines, 2004). Controlled studies of the effect of supraphysiological levels of testosterone on mood and aggression in eugonadal men demonstrate that the majority of men do not experience increases in aggressive feelings or behavior; yet, there is a minority who are affected in becoming more manic than aggressive, suggesting a nonspecific arousal mechanism that may be specific to these men (Anderson et al., 1992; Su et al., 1993; Tricker et al., 1996; Yates et al., 1999; Pope et al., 2000; O'Connor et al., 2004). A meta-analysis of adolescents failed to correlate changing testosterone levels during puberty with associated aggression, in part because most of the studies were cross-sectional (Duke et al., 2014). There have even been studies suggesting that testosterone is primarily involved in status-related behavior (i.e., fairness, protection against social rejection), rather than inducing aggression (Fehr et al., 2010).

Premenopausal women, on the other hand, whose (lower) testosterone levels vary during the menstrual cycle (and who produce a substantial amount of androgens in the adrenals, which are responsive to mood states), may be more responsive in terms of mood and sexual desire to smaller variations in testosterone than are men; postmortem female brains demonstrate greater individual variability in androgen receptor density than male post-mortem brains (Fernandez-Guasti et al., 2000). Sherwin and Gelfand (1985) found that ovariectomized women who received testosterone only, rather than testosterone plus estrogen, estrogen only, or placebo, had significantly higher hostility scores than the other three groups. Two other studies compared violent female cohorts with less violent female cohorts, and found that the more violent women had higher testosterone levels than the less violent women (Ehlers et al., 1980; Dabbs et al., 1988); a third study showed that other androgens in addition to testosterone correlated positively with different measures of aggression (Van der Pahlen et al., 2002). On the other hand, there is no evidence that testosterone therapy in women with conditions of androgen deficiency increases aggression (Glaser and Dimitrakakis, 2013).

In the transgender situation, Van Goozen et al. (1995) reported a study in which thirty-five female-to-male and fifteen male-to-female individuals were evaluated shortly before and three months after the start of cross-gender hormonal treatments. The female-to-male individuals showed an increase in aggression proneness, sexual arousability, and spatial ability. The male-to-female individuals who received cyproterone acetate (an antiandrogen) and estrogen, showed reduced aggression proneness and sexual arousability, and improved verbal ability. On the other hand, Gomez-Gil et al. (2012) report that transexual inpatients undergoing testosterone treatment demonstrated lower levels of social distress, anxiety and depression than patients who had not initiated hormone treatment. It is worth pointing out that because adult men and women undergoing transgender change have undergone fetal development and pubertal development with normative gender hormone and receptor balances in the brain and peripheral tissues, and because there are several potential confounding variables, it is uncertain whether findings in studies such as these can be applied to the cis-gender population.

In summary, we don't yet know enough about testosterone. It functions differently in men from women—during fetal development, during the prepubertal years, during puberty, adulthood, and in later years, particularly for postmenopausal women. We don't know to what degree testosterone determines behavior, and to what degree it reflects behavior caused by numerous other variables—biological and environmental. And as far as I could tell through my literature search, I know of no study that examines biological markers such as androgens in the setting of sexual abuse.

CLINICAL EXPERIENCE

I thought about the people I've seen in my practice, and the fact that I've never seen a man who has admitted to the perpetration of sexual abuse with a child. But I've seen many women who were sexually exploited as children.

Clinical Vignette: 1

> The first such person I worked with early in my career was a seasoned teacher of small children who presented for help with long-standing depression. In the first session, although she didn't mention the idea of physical or emotional abuse and didn't describe anything unusual about her blue-collar family of origin other than the fact that her father liked alcohol, I felt oddly crowded and physically uncomfortable. I found myself wanting to move away from Janice, and although she was demure and respectful in manner, I found her intangibly intrusive. Gradually, over several years, I learned about her horrifying history, in which she was sexually abused by her father, later by male teachers and coaches, then by a priest, and then by a series of male sexual partners. She wasn't seeking help for depression, but for a fragmented sense of identity, disorientation, and an ongoing intermittent loss of contact with reality that characterized her dissociative disorder. There were harrowing sessions in which she presented in unusual clothing, couldn't recall how she had started her day, spoke in a Southern drawl, and attempted to seduce me. Or sessions when I realized she had driven to my office drunk, and I'd require her to wait in my waiting room after the session to be picked up by a friend. Or sessions when she described how she was physically overpowered as a little girl and brilliantly left her body and hovered over the room to escape the pain, rage, helplessness, and terror of the event, leaving me feeling depleted and flattened.
>
> Janice had three biological children in addition to the small children she came to love during the years she had worked as a teacher. Some of the children she taught had been victims of violence, neglect, and complex social circumstances that reminded her of her own early environment. Some of the young boys were already aggressive, and as you can imagine, Janice often felt provoked in her school setting—provoked to be aggressive with highly defended parents, cranky teachers, indifferent administrators, and the aggressive children themselves. However, remarkably to me, she never lost her temper and never struck back with the vengeance she sometimes displayed in my office. How was she able to contain these angry feelings in her everyday life? I think it was through her empathic capacity and internal fluidity, the same fluidity that gave rise to the alters I had met in my office. She could shift from angry retaliator to frightened child in a heartbeat, thus identifying with the vulnerable child, thereby protecting rather than perpetrating. As she later de-

scribed it to me, it was through the experience of giving birth to and raising three children—feeling their movements inside her body, appreciating their complete dependency on her, ministering to their incremental growth and autonomy on a moment-to-moment basis—that she had discovered her protective instinct as a mother. Those seminal experiences, in combination with her positive role in influencing the developments of so many children in school, tipped the balance toward reparation and away from revenge.

Clinical Vignette: 2

Mary, a middle-aged academic, had been intimidated by a stern father, offered up to "high society" men by a defeated mother, sexually abused in childhood by a male neighbor, and then was subjected to a series of compromised dating situations with male partners in adolescence while she was clouded by cocaine and alcohol. During her analysis, we came to understand the lack of safety she felt at home, the scary sexual currents that she felt when working as a cocktail waitress at her neighbor's parties, and the anger she felt along with her flirtatious desire when she related to me from her supine position on the couch. We discussed her pain at not being able to conceive because of endometriosis, and her wish to become a mother to offer a child a different kind of development. Her husband, significantly older, was ambivalent about having children with her, but he ultimately assented to adopting a child. Mary was a capable mother, applying much of what she had learned and internalized in her treatment, but struggled with her daughter's curiosity about her biological mother, which she experienced as a rejection of her special maternal role. Through her experience of me as "not available enough," she was able to work through her anger and to understand her rejection of her own mother, who had failed her in numerous developmental ways. Ultimately, it was through Mary's experience of adoptive motherhood with its gratifications and frustrations—coupled with her transference experiences in treatment that included me as protector—that allowed her to integrate her experiences of having been sexually abused, and to embrace the role of protector rather than avenger in her own life.

My experience as a therapist for a group of female survivors of sexual abuse provided another example of the importance of working through anger, and not just at the perpetrator. The group was comprised of women who had been abused in childhood by men, had been in their own individual therapies for at least one year, and then presented for membership in a group that was to meet once weekly for six months, was to be co-led by a female psychologist and me, and was to be dynamic and exploratory. As expected, I was the target for the rage of these women for the first five months of the group's life: at first, they emphasized the injustice of administration's having stuck them with a male leader; then, they pointed out my insensitive comments and obvious ignorance about abuse; then, they identified my offensive presence in responding to my co-therapist, Danya, and to the members; and finally, they expressed their fear that I could subjugate them, control them, and hurt them as had their male abusers. Finally, to my part-surprise, what emerged in the last month of the group's life was an even greater animosity toward my co-therapist: as toxic as I was, Danya was worse. After all, she seemed to overlook my foibles; she seemed preoccupied and self-absorbed; and she stood by apathetically while her children were being abused. As expected, the group members' childhood experiences of their mother's neglect—and in some cases co-perpetration—came to the fore. The members' ability to express their rage, to integrate their experiences of both parents, to admit their inclination to strike others—including their children—and ultimately to link their past experiences with their new experiences of the therapists, was decisive. By the last session, not only was there substantial insight on the part of members into their bias toward repetition, but several members offered apologies to us for the way they had treated us, with gratitude for our having absorbed their anger, and for helping them to understand their feelings. I will never forget the way the group members organized as they walked out of the room and said goodbye to us: they formed a line, shook our hands, and said goodbye the way a reception line forms and greets a new couple who has just married. I think we *were* a new couple for this group of women; the first parental unit who witnessed their abuse, who tolerated their sadness and anger, and who gave them an opportunity to repair what had been broken within a symbolic familial setting.

A HYPOTHESIS

So, what explains the relatively low incidence of female abuse of children, despite the fact that females—of all ages and in different contexts and cultures—are more commonly abused? I would like to propose that the answer lies in two important differences from males: their defenses and developmental/social roles, both of which follow from their bodily uniqueness. Let us begin with a consideration of the development of defenses.

Female psychological defenses tend to be more fluid. This observation follows from my experience as a practitioner where I have treated numerous adolescent and adult males and females. Elise's (1997) theory of a female's primary sense of femaleness, in which a little girl develops a self-representation built upon a growing knowledge of her vulva and vagina as her special genitals at the interface between inside and outside, is one example of a building block of this fluidity. There are other important differences between girls and boys in early development that bear on the development of their defenses. For one, little girls are maturationally more advanced than boys (Korner, 1973; Olesker, 1990), and they separate from their mothers earlier than do boys during the separation-individuation process (Olesker, 1990). Compatible with these observations, Tronick and Cohn (1989) and Weinberg et al. (1999) found gender differences in six-month-old infants of nondepressed mothers; boys were more affected by their mother's affective communications, while girls demonstrated more self-regulatory behaviors than did boys (Tronick, 2007). Moreover, following from Tronick's mutual regulation model, boys were more vulnerable to their mothers' depressive status, and the depressed mothers experienced them as more burdensome than the girls, thus resulting in greater reciprocal negativity between mothers and sons (Tronick, 2007).

Boys demonstrate more so-called phallic aggression during years two through four than do girls (Parens, 1990). Observational studies of children at preschool ages demonstrate greater measurement of male physical aggression (Potegal and Archer, 2004). Studies also show that with age, girls are more likely to demonstrate anger through turning inward and through crying, while boys are more likely to demonstrate it through action (Vingerhoets and Scheirs, 2000). Studies of latency age children demonstrate that boys are drawn to objects that project outward, while girls show a proclivity for inner spaces (Mayer, 1991). Schiller (2012) points out that girls prefer spinning games, as opposed to boys' preference for linear, thrusting games. Hay (2007) summarizes the literature, and hypothesizes that boys begin to differentiate from girls in their propensity for aggression after the age of two based on the following principles: girls mature earlier than boys and are more prepared for civilized socialization; measured group gender differences are heavily influenced by boys who have emotional and cognitive problems and resort to aggression because of them, and boys are at higher risk for these problems than girls; girls and boys tend to segregate into gendered social worlds during childhood, and boys are more likely to play roughly, while girls are more likely to be aggressive verbally, especially with friends. Putting these observations together, a picture begins to emerge: generally speaking, small boys are more clingy and sensitive to their mothers' mood states, and they are more inclined to respond to their mood states through action turned outward. Girls, because of their growing sense of the importance of their internal spaces, and their reidentification with their mothers and their mothers' bodies (Balsam, 1996), have a more fluid relationship between inside and outside, and have a more internalized orientation toward their feeling states.

Let us now consider what happens to the female body later in the life cycle. I think that a woman's experience of menstruating on a monthly basis, from the time she reaches puberty through menopause, becomes a core part of her self-experience. So does the impact of hormonal variations on her moods, which she experiences as rapid, powerful, and autonomous. I think this experience may leave adult female patients more tolerant of affective shifts, of exploration for causes of those shifts, and more open to the possibility that there may not exist definitive explanations for those shifts. I also think that the regular flow of blood out of her body reinforces the fact that the gap between inside and outside is permeable.

Then there is the matter of a woman's participation in pregnancy and early childcare. Until fairly recently, the significance of pregnancy in the development of a woman's self-concept has been underestimated within the analytic field. We now recognize that a woman's carrying a child for nine months has a profound effect on her sense of femaleness, on her perception of her body—its generative potential, its power, its sensations as the fetus grows within her, and its elasticity—and on her relationship with her own mother. That experience, together with childbirth and her experience of bringing an infant into the sphere of the primary maternal attachment, is transformative. This is an experience that fathers do not have. It is also true that in Western culture, women provide the majority of the pre-Oedipal oxygen, as infants grow into mobile talking toddlers, and then into school-age autonomous small people. The field of child observation has understandably focused on the developmental nuances of the child, but perhaps not sufficiently on the impact of this process on mothers. I would argue that the responsibility of attending to the care of a small child, immersion in the primary attachment milieu with that child, and helping that child to establish self-object differentiation, along with additional developmental steps, allow the mother to work through her own primary attachment process yet again, with the possibility for ongoing repair. My work with female analysis and and women committed to in-depth psychotherapies, in which they have described their maternal experiences, has supported this claim. What is the impact of this mothering experience when it goes well? I would argue that, on the whole, the capacity for a mother's mentalization is deepened. Frustration tolerance is strengthened, and the delay between impulse and action is widened. The awareness of the separateness between self and object is increased, along with the appreciation for how fine the line between self and object often is.

However, there are many instances in which caring for a child doesn't go well. A mother's troubled internalized object relationships, early developmental trauma, or adverse circumstances at the time of motherhood—such as psychosocial strain or depression—can compromise her ability to care for her child. In particular, if that mother has been sexually abused as a child, she is at greater risk for abusing her own child. This would explain why the female sexual offenders I spoke about earlier are themselves the most severe victims: they have high rates of violence and incest in their own family histories, they have higher rates of psychopathology when examined as adults, and—in their abuse of adolescents—they are not very aware that adolescents are actually large children. Male abusers, on the other hand, don't seem to have been maligned as badly as children; they are often mistreated and neglected, but not victimized physically as often. Yet, they are more often the perpetrators of abuse, and epidemiologic data strongly suggests that dysregulated anger and hostility correlate with male sexual offending (Ahmed, 2014). In summary, I am proposing that women may be immunized by their experience as mothers, but only to a degree; when they are overwhelmingly traumatized as children, they are vulnerable to becoming abusers themselves, and their internalized bad objects compromise their ability to empathize with their victims.

FUTURE DIRECTIONS

I have tried in this discussion to combine observations from the consulting room with epidemiological data and with knowledge gathered from other related disciplines. I think this approach is a fertile one and takes advantage of several different perspectives to study the problem of sexual exploitation. Therapists can only learn about one precious narrative at a time, and it is important for us to share our stories and to speak with other experts who have collected information about sexual trauma so that we can protect our fellow human beings from injuring each other.

What kind of additional psychological studies could add to our knowledge base? For one, it would be helpful to know more about the etiology of physical abuse. Just how does the neglect of young boys result in such high rates of sexual abuse and violence perpetrated by those children when they develop into young men? What are the important variables that determine the movement from being hurt to hurting the other, especially in males? How can we soothe the pain of those—more often females—who have been hurt and who direct the pain most typically toward themselves? What other public health interventions can be planned that would take advantage of our psychological understanding, since it is unlikely that we will be able to offer excellent psychotherapy to all members of the population who have been injured? How can we help people to develop their empathic capacities outside of the consulting room, especially targeting the boys who have been hurt/neglected and go on later to injure vulnerable children? Our own Henri Parens has been an exemplar for this kind of public education through his work educating parents about the vicissitudes of aggression during childhood development (Parens, 2011). These questions and many others follow from the public health problem of sexual abuse.

Chapter Six

The Culture of Sex Trafficking

Vivian Pender

Sex trafficking is the buying and selling of persons for the purpose of sexual exploitation. It is defined by an *act*, a *means*, and a *purpose*: the *act* of harboring, recruiting, or transporting a person by *means* of force, fraud, or coercion for the *purpose* of sexual exploitation. Since children under the age of eighteen cannot legally consent to have sex with an adult, evidence of force, fraud, or coercion is not necessary to prove trafficking in the case of children. Although sex trafficking is a human rights violation and a crime that happens in virtually every country in the world, not until 2000 did the world community meet to set forth an international agreed-upon definition of sexual exploitation. The Palermo Protocol, as it is informally known, is an international treaty to prevent, suppress, and punish trafficking in persons especially women and children, supplementing the United Nations Convention against Transnational Organized Crime. Article 3, paragraph (a) of the Protocol

> defines Trafficking in Persons as the recruitment, transportation, transfer, harbouring or receipt of persons, by means of the threat or use of force or other forms of coercion, of abduction, of fraud, of deception, of the abuse of power or of a position of vulnerability or of the giving or receiving of payments or benefits to achieve the consent of a person having control over another person, for the purpose of exploitation. Exploitation shall include, at a minimum, the exploitation of the prostitution of others or other forms of sexual exploitation, forced labour or services, slavery or practices similar to slavery, servitude or the removal of organs. (United Nations Human Rights Protocol to Prevent, Suppress and Punish Trafficking in Persons Especially Women and Children, Supplementing the United Nations Convention Against Transnational Organized Crime 2015)

Also in 2000, the United States passed the Victims of Trafficking and Violence Protection Act:

> To combat trafficking in persons, especially into the sex trade, slavery, and involuntary servitude, to reauthorize certain Federal programs to prevent violence against women, and for other purposes." (2000, p. 1466)

This act was reauthorized every few years, however, it received limited funding. More recently, in 2015, the U.S. Justice for Victims of Trafficking Act was passed. It increases direct services, compensation, and restitution for victims of trafficking and child pornography. It enhances services for runaway and homeless youth. It also seeks to enhance reporting and reduce the demand for sex trafficking. The designation "prostitute" has been changed to "prostituted person," emphasizing passive victimization rather than active criminality. Accompanying this, the criminal focus has shifted from the prostituted person to the buyer and the trafficker.

Sex trafficking does not exist in isolation nor have random attempts to reduce its destructive effects been successful. Rather, it is perpetuated in longstanding cultures of patriarchy, legalized prostitution, pervasive pornography, domestic and interpersonal violence, and rampant sexual abuse. Sex trafficking is a reflection and a product of these worldwide aspects of cultures and depends on three essential elements: the victim, the buyer, and the trafficker. In this model, demand for commercial sexual service is the main driver of sex trafficking although the buyer has not been the focus of investigation until now. While more has been written about the victim of trauma, less of the psychoanalytic literature has been directed to the perpetrators, the buyer, and the trafficker. Most authors of books and journal articles are criminologists or sociologists. This chapter attempts to address some of these shortcomings, provide a more inclusive view of sex trafficking, and establish a new psychoanalytical framework in order to better understand the individuals involved and the culture. With this increased awareness, action may be taken to begin to address abusive treatment of disenfranchised groups in the context of a general culture.

At first, thinking about sex trafficking is difficult. It represents one of the worst examples of human behavior and victimization; however, it is insinuated in our general culture more than is acknowledged. It can be found in such places as nail salons, truck stops, hotels, professional conferences, markets, and the Super Bowl. And the tendrils go deeper than most will consciously admit. For example, buyers come from all socioeconomic levels; they may be manual laborers, soldiers, celebrities, judges, or physicians. Thus, it is important to raise awareness and explore the implicit cultural meanings pervasive in societies in which sex trafficking exists. If commercialization and sexual enslavement of vulnerable persons is unthinkable, it is also unspeakable. Yet sexual exploitation has been a phenomenon of human culture since recorded time. And it has appeared in different forms, for example, illegal child marriage and legalized brothels. The legalization of prostitution found in these forms exists in about fifty countries, including the United States. Most recently, it has been found in refugee and migrant camps where there is a breakdown of law enforcement.

Since sex trafficking includes other domains such as law, government, politics, health, and economics, it is important to be aware of the broader cultural environment that overlaps with sex trafficking. There are universal themes in various areas of the culture of sex trafficking that are based on a foundation of power, violence, prejudice, and abuse of certain individuals whose identity, class, or gender subject them to inherent biases and attitudes. The following statistics give some idea of the scope of sex trafficking:

- The International Labor Organization estimates that 21 million people are victims of human trafficking and forced labor, with 5.5 million of that number being children.
- The U.S. Human Trafficking Reporting System found that 82 percent of incidents of human trafficking were classified as sex trafficking, and 83 percent of sex trafficking victims in the U.S. were American citizens, while 87 percent of sex trafficking victims were younger than twenty-five years of age.
- Although boys are trafficked, the majority of those trafficked for commercial sex are women and girls.
- The ILO estimates that $99 billion is derived from the commercial sex industry. Sex trafficking is more lucrative than labor trafficking, organ trafficking, and the trafficking of drugs and arms. That is, more money can be made from the multiple sales of a body as a commodity.
- Sex trafficked people are exploited much more frequently within their own borders.
- Human trafficking has been reported in all fifty U.S. states.
- U.S.-regulated brothels are legal in some counties in the state of Nevada.
- In 2016, the National Hotline Trafficking Resource Center (NHTRC) hotline received over 20,000 calls resulting in identification of 7,572 individual victims.

To summarize, sex trafficking as a financial industry depends on supply and demand, high reward and low risk, and systemic inequalities. Systemic inequalities (push and pull factors) are, for example, poverty, lack of education, lack of access to health care, lack of child protection systems, systems of discrimination, and displacement due to conflict or natural disasters that make people vulnerable and more susceptible to being exploited and/or trafficked. Other physical, cognitive, or emotional impairments result in vulnerabilities for sexual exploitation. Most sex trafficking is heterosexual, that is, between a male buyer and a female victim. Children victims are mostly girls, but boys are certainly victims as well. The following sections of this chapter will elaborate the vicissitudes of sex trafficking as it applies to the victims, the buyers, and the traffickers. It will also include some clinical treatments and a research project.

Some individuals involved in sex trafficking include the following:

- Parents who sell or give their children to traffickers.
- Parents who act as traffickers for their children.
- Children who grow up in brothels.
- Child brides in the United States and other countries.
- Sex tourism, which is especially prevalent in Southeast Asia.
- Children adopted for the purpose of gain from pornography or sex.
- Children kidnapped to be used for labor or sex.
- Children kidnapped to be used as child soldiers.
- Adolescents, especially runaways, picked up by gangs.
- State-sponsored rape as a means of genocide or to provide sexual service for government soldiers

In long-held patriarchal traditions, men dominate top levels of society's institutions. A glaring example of this is present in medical academics. Although medical school classes in 2018 are composed of 50 percent women, the percentage drops at higher professorial ranks. Women make up 46 percent of assistant professors, 38 percent of associate professors, and 23 percent of full professors. Similar rankings are found in psychoanalytic institutes and societies. For example, the International Psychoanalytical Association, after more than one hundred years, elected its first female president in 2017.

THE VICTIMS

At a conference in 2015, in Milwaukee, of law enforcement, mental health providers, and trafficking survivors, one survivor said, "Each time I was raped, a little piece of me died. Sometimes it was my pimp, but more often, men I didn't know. After a while, there were no more pieces left. I was already dead. I was so broken it took me more than twenty years to escape" (personal communication).

A major flaw in the Palermo Protocol is the emphasis on the physical rather than the psychological. Although sex trafficking encompasses both physical and psychological traumas, the harm to the victim is due primarily to the long-lasting psychic destruction of complex trauma. The physicality plays a role in actualizing the psyche, rather than when one deals with merely fantasies. The terms "force, fraud, or coercion" have psychological meaning beyond their legal implications. In fact, many victims, due to the shame they feel, will not admit to being coerced. A child who is always the object of people in their environment can easily be forced or fraudulently coerced into a chronic behavior, even as destructive as abuse. Many cultures groom girls for a range of eventual abuse. Girls, more often than boys, are frequently taught to be compliant and this sets the stage for their potential vulnerability in childhood as well as later in adulthood. The World Health Organization (2015) reported that 35 percent of women have experienced either intimate known partner violence and/or unknown non-partner violence. In intimate partner violence, the perpetrators are few, and results in psychological depression in the victim. In repeated unknown non-partner sexual violence, the result in the victim is fear and dissociation. Psychoanalysis, with its extensive literature on the psychic consequences of trauma and abuse, has in this light much to contribute to an understanding of what may lead to sex trafficking.

Those women and children involved with a trafficker (who could be a family member) are eventually psychologically sex trafficked. Escape is almost impossible. There are many forms of sex service, (countries that have legalized prostitution have online menus) from streetwalking to stripping, from brothels to in-house, from live sex shows to sex workers. Children may be involved in any of these venues. The web has made procurement of sex services significantly streamlined and easy. All should be considered under the category of sex trafficked. There does not have to be movement of the victim from one place to another; children and other vulnerable groups can be victimized online. Usually it is more than one incident; a form of repeated violence is likely to have occurred. After that, the mere threat of violence is enough to maintain the victim in her role. Often there are *no* physical restraints—imprisonment is psychological.

The average age of initiation into sex trafficking is twelve years old. A history of neglect and sexual abuse is usually found. Children who are under the age of twelve are malleable, those made weak by starvation, and those who are maimed or given drugs are exploited for sex. Elisabeth Young-Bruehl (2010) surveyed shifts in understanding of sexual diversity. She emphasized how thinking in terms of three sexual binaries—male/female, masculine/feminine, same sex/opposite sex—preference has receded. She correlated these shifts with greater understanding around the world of the complexities of sex and sexual behavior and with studies of prejudice that emphasize the importance of defensive group identities requiring ascetic practice in the development of intolerance for sexual diversity. She suggested a redefinition of sexual pathology in terms of the abusive quality of pathological relationships rather than in the older terms of deviancy or perversion. She uses an example of pedophilia discussed as an abusive relationship with a child involving prejudice against children which she names "childism."

In a webinar on sex trafficking, Fischer (2015) noted this:

> The impact of the initial trauma of rape followed by sexual trafficking leaves children in a state of physiological and psychological hyper-arousal and disorganization with a tendency to dissociation and the development of complex trauma with flashbacks that disrupt ego functioning. This leads to avoidance, numbing, painful mood, hyper-vigilance, distrust, fears, separation and annihilation anxieties, nightmares, developmental anomalies and developmental arrests. It affects affect regulation so that she is either overwhelmed with feeling or saddled with the pressing defensive need to turn off all feeling. There are disturbances of attachment, conduct, concentration, cognitive and academic dysfunction, self-doubts, depression, low self-esteem, an overall sense of helplessness. There are also endocrinologic, immunologic and neurologic as well as psychological changes. There can be a complete breakdown of ability to cope resulting in rage, passivity, helplessness and hopelessness. Food and sleep may be restricted, movement is limited and she is subjected to erratic verbal and physical abuse. This diminishes her sense of self, increases her difficulty with trust and leads to the Stockholm Syndrome, in which she defends, identifies with and loves the abuser whom she experiences as her savior. Temporary effective coping mechanisms such as passivity, denial, numbing, and dissociation, ultimately yield to maladaptive patterns and character mechanisms of defense that impair development and consign these girls to a future of bondage. (Webinar: Human Trafficking: Training Healthcare)

Pornography, also a universal fixture in almost every culture, plays a role in sex education. On average, boys are around thirteen years of age, and girls are around fourteen, when they first see pornography, according to Bryant Paul (cited in Jones, 2018), an associate professor at Indiana University's Media School and the author of many studies on porn content and adolescent and adult viewing habits. Many of the heterosexual videos are shot from the male point of view, as if the man were holding the camera while he has sex with a woman whose main job, via oral sex, intercourse, or anal sex, is to make him orgasm. Pornography is also a gateway to sex trafficking.

> In law, consent is defined as a voluntary agreement with an action proposed by another. Here is another instance where legal or medical definitions can be enhanced by psychoanalysis. "Consent is an act of reason; the person giving consent must be of sufficient mental capacity and be in possession of all essential information in order to give valid consent. A person who is an infant, is mentally incompetent, or is under the influence of drugs is incapable of giving consent. Consent must also be free of coercion or fraud. Informed consent of a [medical] patient or other recipient of services based on the principles of autonomy and privacy; this has become the requirement at the center of morally valid decision making in health care and research. Seven criteria define informed consent: (1) competence to understand and to decide,

> (2) voluntary decision making, (3) disclosure of material information, (4) recommendation of a plan, (5) comprehension of terms (3) and (4), (6) decision in favor of a plan, and (7) authorization of the plan. A person gives informed consent only if all of these criteria are met. If all of the criteria are met except that the person rejects the plan, that person makes an informed refusal." (Medical Dictionary, 2015)

This legal definition, widely used in health care and medicine, does not take into account an understanding of developmental attitudes and psychic meaning. From a psychoanalytic perspective, one may ask if a female who develops in an intersectional mapping of multiple abusive identities can have informed consent of the use of her body. At the time of her first sexual encounter, it is not clear that a female adolescent is capable of volitional consent. In this context, and the culture in which a girl matures, can a woman truly have agency of her body? Perhaps the attention that many women ordinarily pay to their adornment and physique are defenses against the realization that they have lost agency of their bodies. They may also be imbued with confusing guilt from using their objectified bodies. One would expect that a woman may have so many unconscious biases that she may not be able to speak for herself. She may indeed use her body for what she thinks is self-preservation only to later find herself, as in commercial sex, destroyed by others' exploitation of her (Valenti, 2016).

THE BUYERS

There is almost no literature on buyers. Resources report some men in the United States experience high rates of sex with prostituted persons and associated practices such as pornography, strip clubs, erotic massage, sexual touching, and other forms of commercial sex. The numbers would predict a high rate in men. If every prostituted woman has an average of eight encounters a night, there are that many more buyers than victims.

There is significant literature on masculinity. Corbett (2009a) reexamined Freud's "Analysis of a Phobia in a Five-Year-Old Boy." He discussed Hans's construction and acts of consciousness that continue to endow the psychoanalytic construct of masculinity with meaning. Corbet suggests that Freud moved in his discussion of the case to regulate the unsettled conditions of masculinity that he articulated through his clinical observations. The case of Hans is viewed as an exemplary illustration of how masculinity is foretold—a normative narrative that has changed little in the last 100 years, although recently "destructive" masculinities are being examined. Corbett (2009b) offers a contemporary view of masculinity as a dilemma of boundary—neither fully interior nor fully exterior, neither fully fantastic nor fully socially constructed. It is unclear if what is expected from masculinity can be used to understand why men engage in violent sex. The buyer of sex is under the illusion that the activity is consensual but he may easily become violent.

Malarek (2011), a journalist, noted that most men do not think about the reality of prostitution. They may rationalize that it is "easy money" or "she enjoys it" or "no one is being hurt" or it was a "choice" to be in what has been called a profession. One possible way of considering it a profession is to profess knowledge of the sexual needs of men that is the fantasy of being all knowing about them. The buyers deny that the woman has to act perversely as if she is enjoying the sexual encounter.

Malarek went on to comment about why some men buy sex. Many are frustrated with their domestic partners or wives. Some find a mystique of the exotic "Other," a different race for example, exciting. Freud (1912) famously highlighted the Madonna-whore complex, the psychic impotence in males who envision women as either saints or prostitutes. He wrote, "Where such men love they have no desire and where they desire they cannot love" (p. 183). He believed that these men hated their mothers, who were cold and controlling. They sought a maternal relationship but became frustrated thereby reviving their incestuous ties. The prostituted women are containers for the men's maternal sadistic hatred.

Freud (1912) provided a link from sexual acts to the maternal experience. Ordinarily the sexual act under any circumstance includes nudity, tactile sensations, and bodily secretions, regressive primitive features that can be traced to an early time in life with one's mother (or her representation). In addition to a natural desire, how sex is performed depends on social and cultural norms and contexts. A clinical case will provide some details.

Clinical Vignette: 1

> Ronald, an intelligent successful businessman, age fifty-five years old, came to treatment with me for his panic attacks and bouts of anger that took the form of uncontrolled rage. He became easily enraged with any number of slights but especially those that seemed to come from women. He experienced his mother as cold while demanding obedience at home, church, and school. She beat him when he disobeyed her. He reported a current incident. A woman in a coffee shop who cut in front of him while standing in line so infuriated him that he began yelling at her and called her offensive slurs, such as "bitch." People initially stepped back but then spoke up, and Ronald stopped the avalanche of his verbal abuse. However, he continued to feel angry, and so he took the piece of gum he was chewing and as he walked past her was able to smash it into her fur coat without her noticing. The oral symbolism did not go unnoticed. His loneliness was profound. His only intimate relationships were with prostituted women. There were a few women whom he invited regularly to go for a week with him to resorts or skiing. He considered these women companions, girlfriends, and well-compensated. He was sure they enjoyed themselves. He could enjoy any kind of orifice sex while fantasizing about rape, but his main

> source of pleasure was being in control of the women, the relationship, and his sexual pleasure. He wanted dominance over women and could only have that with a prostituted woman.

Birch (2015), a criminologist, in his book, *Why Men Buy Sex*, remarks on human sexuality and the context of procurement and notes that nonsexual behaviors are a large part of sex. If one looks at the larger context, it is apparent and applies to sex purchased from a prostituted person. Psychic needs are perhaps the most obvious in nonsexual behaviors. Some of these behaviors include those associated with conventional dating and romantic relationships rather than deviant behavior. Birch's research found that with singular or first time sexual procurement, the focus is on the sex act itself. He reasons that most men who continue to procure sex find positive factors to engage in the practice. Religious groups have tended to be pejorative and prohibitive of female sexuality, thereby casting a morally conservative verdict. Thus, as an underground activity, sexual procurement became associated with crime, although most recently, similar to drug abuse, the victims of drugs and sex trafficking are being diverted to treatment rather than jails and prisons.

The legalization of prostitution as a social experiment has not improved matters in the opinions of several contributors to the field (Moran, 2013; Farley, 2015). They note that it would be rare for a girl to want to grow up to be a prostituted person. Women who are given a choice of an income earning usual occupation do not choose to be prostituted for sex. It is associated with lack of agency, control, and risk for physical abuse. However, the man who procures sex for money does not consciously think of the victim, instead he imagines that the relationship has other benefits, even romantic ones. The prostituted woman has no such illusions. She knows that she cannot fulfill the procurer's fantasies and that they are not real. In fact, she is in the business of making herself merely appear to be enjoying him and his attention. The fantasy that the relationship can be anything more than a commercial transaction does not exist for the prostituted woman. In the best of circumstances where the woman is protected from violence, she is still however acting a role. When asked, many buyers denied this.

THE TRAFFICKERS

A trafficker is virtually synonymous with the more common and colloquial term "pimp," especially if force, fraud, and coercion are considered from a psychological perspective. Psychoanalytic literature exploring a psychic understanding of traffickers or "pimps" is almost nonexistent. They can only be partially understood through documentaries. In *Tricked: The Documentary* (2013), one of the opening scenes shows a trafficker who says, "There are two kinds of pussy. One you give away and one you sell. Now why wouldn't you want to sell it?" he asks in a self-evidentiary rhetorical question. The documentary does not distinguish between traffickers and pimps.

> Another pimp said he found his girls at a bar or online by casually chatting with them. He tested them by asking them to do something for him that was extraordinary. One example was to ask her for the keys to her car after speaking for fifteen minutes. If she did this without question and little reassurance, he took this as a clue that she would do other things for him. He thought it worked most of the time. He enjoyed going to the "Player's Ball," a regular event in the U.S. that awards the "Pimp of the Year" [reserved for male pimps] with a trophy-like Player's Cup. (Pender, 2017, p. 22)

There are a few mostly unpublished papers on perpetrators of incest that can be used to extrapolate the relationship between the victim and her trafficker. In both, incest and sex trafficking, the perpetrator's assault on the girl's reality testing intensifies her self-doubt and ego impairment. In one form, this emanates from the trafficker who, while taking over her mind, body, and integrity, manipulates her into believing that he alone cares for her. He attains his goal through psychological coercion. He establishes an environment of chronic stress threatening, provoking fear, intensifying her sense of disconnection thru isolation and ultimately creating a sense of helplessness.

Just as incestuous sex attempts to negate loss, incompleteness, and ambivalence for the perpetrator of incest, the same is true for the trafficker of prostituted sex. Difference between the sexes is made to appear as if it is nonconflicted and can therefore be denied. Tesone's papers (2003, 2005) presented at International Psychoanalytical Association conferences on incest are useful as an extrapolation of trafficking. The girl-child in both situations suffered from maternal neglect and fatherly absence. In prostitution, "Daddy" as the pimp is frequently called, serves as a distorted caretaker. Particularly if the prostituted woman's trajectory frequently began as a child and her relationship with her trafficker can be considered incestuous.

Tesone further remarked that his patient who had been imprisoned, tortured, and raped had felt pleasure at the moment of vaginal penetration. In her case, her pleasure may be understood in relation to her circumstances. Any attention that was personal and not too brutal could have been experienced as pleasurable. This may be true of the neglected girl child as well. His patient had been molested from age three to age seven by her grandfather, whom she loved, with fellatio and vaginal penetration with his fingers. The shame she felt was caused not by her pleasure but by her knowledge that this was wrong, immoral, and abusive. If he was gentle, it tickled her, but if he was rough, it hurt. Even as a child, she absorbed the guilt of her grandfather's exploitation. If she had pleasure, it was in whatever positive emotions he offered and the child's reflection of his approval of her. Her mother dismissed her competitive claims that the mother's father was attentive to her in this way.

Perpetrators of incest are much like the traffickers who steal the excitement of the victim. Sharing her with the sex buyers is consistent with the noninclusive relationship that incest provides. Similar psychodynamics apply to the almost half of traffickers who are women. Neither the trafficker nor the buyer nor the prostituted person can symbolize such traumatizing and alienating events. Continuity of life is disrupted by this destruction of a human and a human relationship. None of the persons have true agency. Deriving sexual pleasure from experiencing another human as a nonexistent object does not infuse the trafficker or the buyer with emotional growth and energy, rather it drains them. Denial of reality consumes a great deal of energy in order to maintain the defense mechanism. Repetition however unfulfilling is required as demonstrated by the recurring behavior of sex buyers. In addition to the abused body, the abusing body also becomes the object of shame, scorn, and antithesis of life. Flesh is potentially damaged in the process with the potential for sexually transmitted diseases. However, an illusion of possessing the woman all to himself may prevail for the moment with the buyer and in the longer relationship with the trafficker. Another clinical case may be useful as an extrapolation.

Clinical Vignette: 2

Jack, an attorney, sixty years old, was married to Jane, who was thirty-one years old. He saw her as having the attractiveness that his older sister had and envied her femininity. An image of his youthful sister, substituted by Jane, seemed to him an imagined return to being young again. He thought of himself as hypermasculine, enjoying hunting, and being a dominating force in litigation. He prided his collection of cars that he owned. He thought it was important for a man to own things such as cars and women. He reported having had a difficult relationship with his mother, whom he experienced as excessively hypercritical. Jane's parents divorced when she was young and she rarely saw her father throughout her childhood. Jack enjoyed her dependency on him, her passivity, and lack of education. He also identified with her girlish femininity and wanted to help her financially, although he was offended when she referred to him as a "sugar daddy." He felt all-powerful with her, thereby appearing as if he had control over time and death.

After some time, Jack began to lose his positive feelings for Jane. He reported that he could not relate to her. What had originally been an exciting lustful relationship, dwindled to a nonintimate relationship. It appeared that Jane began having sexual affairs with other men, while Jack's primary sexual activity was masturbation with fantasies of omnipotent powerful women dominating him. This was interpreted in the transference. Interestingly, Jack was not upset by his wife's affairs and there was some conjecture that they represented his own homosexual interests. Proud of his promiscuous behaviors as a young man, he was now distraught. He began driving to an area of town where the streetwalking sex workers performed oral sex. It was a way that he could feel more powerful over women again. In his analysis, his behaviors were interpreted in relation to the transference. He called his female analyst a "cunt," and at one point, treatment had to be interrupted because he threatened her with physical harm. However, after divorcing his wife, he returned to analysis and continues in treatment ten years later with significantly less rage toward women and a subsequent relationship with a woman he shared many attributes.

Although Jack was not in reality a trafficker, some of his behaviors and phantasies were analogous. He demonstrated the need to control and be all-powerful with women. He acted this out with his younger, dependent, less-experienced and less-educated wife. He procured sex from her and from prostituted women to maintain his sense of masculinity. The sexual activity he enjoyed the most was when he could act out the fantasy of being a baby, completely dependent for food, nurturance, and cleaning. In his fantasies, he sometimes enjoyed being bound by ropes while he was vigorously and sadistically cleaned with a harsh cloth.

Ronald and Jack are the closest clinical examples in psychoanalytic treatments that illustrate theories about the trafficker—and, perhaps, the buyer—while having sex with a child. Psychoanalysts can extrapolate a good deal of theoretical understanding from real incestuous relationships. With incest, the procurers feel ownership as well as a lack of differentiation between him and the child, similar to the prostituted woman. The mothers of these men are reported to be sadistically controlling and cold. They felt their existence was solely for the purpose of ownership without regard to the living, feeling, experiencing, and developing child that they were. They frequently felt non-existent but they enacted the reversal of this relationship with prostituted women and children. There was no confusion for them; their treatment as a child was unambiguous. As victims themselves, they were silenced. It is that silence that surrounds incest and sex trafficking.

Moreover, it is estimated that there are almost an equal number of woman traffickers as men traffickers. They are usually former prostituted women who have "aged out" of "the life." In an example of a woman trafficker's case, several members of a family were reported to have sexually abused her and she became a woman brothel owner. Traffickers often recruit additional women to offer reassurance and grooming of younger women or children. Some are known to have a mental illness such as a substance abuse disorder. Substances of abuse are a large part of commercial sex trafficking. Substances are used in a variety of ways. Stimulants are given to victims to stay awake and work long hours. Depressants such as alcohol and heroin are used to dull pain and subdue the victim. Substances of abuse are common in buyers and traffickers. They decrease inhibition as well as enhance pleasure.

Other drugs such as Viagra are frequently used to maintain penile erection and prolong a male sexual experience. Otherwise, there is very little in depth knowledge about traffickers who are women.

THE "INDEPENDENT" SEX WORKERS

Even the legal sex worker can be found to have a childhood history that is rife with abuse for adult sexual enjoyment. The sex worker might seek to rationalize their abuse to legitimize identity as an experience. It is as if the sex worker is thinking, "Abuse happened to me for a reason. I was able but now I can be the one in control, use sex as a caring activity, identify with the vulnerability of the buyer and care for the buyer as a [self-representation]." One example is the sex worker who provides sexual services for the disabled homebound person and thinks of his work as a profession for the "greater good." Such sex workers, a small but vocal group, formed the International Union of Sex Workers, a legally recognized organization, based in the United Kingdom (Pender, 2016).

TREATMENT

Most reports of psychoanalytic treatments are of the victim. Ávila and Domínguez (2014) demonstrated the potential changes in a victim of prostitution with relational psychotherapeutic techniques based on the work of Ferenczi. Their paper explores the change processes that took place in a woman, an ex-prostitute, in the context of psychotherapeutic treatment over a period of over three years. The treatment took place within a relational psychotherapeutic setting influenced by the ideas formulated by Sándor Ferenczi regarding trauma, as well as by his intense involvement with and commitment to his patients, as expressed in his *Clinical Diary* (1932). Zoe, the current patient, was a woman born in Latin America who migrated to Spain at the age of twenty-eight and became trapped, for nearly a decade, in a mesh of prostitution networks. She eventually entered regular psychotherapeutic treatment at the age of thirty-nine. Her change process is an example of the mutual influence between the factors of resilience that characterized her and the opportunity for co-creation that the treatment signifies. The marks of the intense traumatic burden of Zoe's history and the rays of sunlight and hope that she is currently experiencing become intermingled in the dreams evoked and brought to the treatment setting. Zoe's capacity for resilience and the potential for founding self-object relations, ethically implied, that therapists can offer construct a scenario that brings back to life the essence of Ferenczi from 1932.

Besides the contribution of Ávila and Domínguez (2014), three other papers need mention: (i) Bennett-Murphy (2012) discusses her treatment of a child survivor of human trafficking and the child's struggle for physical refuge and psychological safety. She remarked on the child's disturbance in her development, relationships and community and the struggle to find refuge, (ii) Kleinschmidt (2009) reported a psychotherapeutic treatment with a teenage mother following human trafficking. The girl had escaped from imprisonment, torture and forced prostitution. She was then trafficked to another country. Her evocative title, "Keeping Mother Alive," has multiple meanings for the adolescent girl, her infant, the treatment and the analyst as well as the concept of the ordinary good mother, and (iii) Orange (2017) examines the ways in which embracing a "psychology of being human" furthers our ability to understand how the intergenerational effects of societal cataclysms, such as those associated with the Holocaust, slavery, and combat, form the contexts of many therapeutic relationships. This model of an individual's relationship with another contributes to our understanding and insight of the relationships between the victim, buyer and trafficker.

RESEARCH

A research project is currently in progress at Weill Cornell Medical College in New York. As noted earlier, evidence of human trafficking in the United States has been documented in all fifty states, involving both adults as well as minors. However, compared to international data, domestic trafficking victims in the United States are much more likely to be minors and young adults, U.S. citizens or legal residents, and more likely victims of sex trafficking, which involves the recruitment, harboring, transportation, provision or obtaining of a person for the purpose of a commercial sex act or commercial sexual exploitation.

During the period they are being trafficked, it is estimated that the vast majority of sex trafficking victims come into contact with healthcare providers. For example, in one study of 107 survivors of sex trafficking in the United States, 88 percent had contact with one or more health professionals during the period of time they were being trafficked. Several studies have characterized the broad range of health consequences that rise from sex work and trafficking, which include sexually transmitted diseases and infections, reproductive health problems, unwanted pregnancies and complications from unsafe or coerced abortions, physical violence and trauma, and mental health problems. During these healthcare visits, most of them do not result in identification of trafficking victims and subsequent referral to appropriate services that allow them to escape their traffickers. Despite evidence of these missed opportunities, few studies have explored the interactions in healthcare settings themselves that influence identification of victims and appropriate linkage to critical assistance.

The purpose of this qualitative study is to explore the values, beliefs, attitudes, and behaviors that influence the behaviors and shapes the experiences of domestic sex trafficking victims in healthcare settings. This project would lay the foundations for understanding how best to shape these healthcare experiences for trafficking victims to better identify victims, improve outreach, and provide critical services to this highly vulnerable population.

Victims of trafficking, and in particular, domestic minor sex trafficking victims (under the age of eighteen), are a vulnerable population that repeatedly seeks health care services, but are not easily identified, and are often referred to inadequate services that allow victims to remain in exploitative environments with their traffickers. Despite insights garnered from the literature studying the health problems and health-care-seeking behavior of other similar vulnerable populations such as victims of intimate partner violence, other forms of trafficking, and commercial sex workers, there is still a limited understanding of domestic minor sex trafficking victims. This gap in understanding is especially true for their experiences and interactions with health care providers. Through our research study, we hope to propose a new theoretical framework for understanding the interpersonal dynamics between healthcare providers and victims of domestic minor sex trafficking, and to characterize the experiences with healthcare providers and the barriers and opportunities for more effective assistance escaping their traffickers during these encounters.

The investigators are an internist, a child psychiatrist, and an adult psychiatrist/psychoanalyst. Over the course of about one year, we have met with focus groups at GEMS (Girls Education and Mentoring Services), a three hundred-bed community facility for sex trafficking survivors in New York. At this time, preliminary data shows the majority of the individuals to be either African American, Hispanic, or mixed. The average age is eighteen years old. They have no viable home to which they can return. They exhibited many characteristics of complex trauma such as hypervigilance, hostility, fragmented identity, depression, and depersonalization. They reported on their experiences with health care. They were interested mostly in being heard and respected otherwise their expectations appear to be minimal.

CONCLUSION

Attitudes that are transmitted from one generation to the next are imbedded in the fabric of the deeper cultural unconscious. They are not easily changed. The prevalence of child abuse, incest, domestic violence, sexual harassment, pornography, and commercial sex, all of which are related to sex trafficking, is evidence of implicit cultural acceptance. One might suspect that there are opposing forces that serve to maintain these practices. The relatively recent laws and international agreements demonstrate a possible change in cultural mores.

Is violence against women de facto violence against children? Children are often considered in many domains to be in a separate category. However, women are often associated with children either by giving birth to them or taking care of them in other ways. Moreover, many trafficked women begin to be trafficked when they were children. Most women who are prostituted have children; sometimes it is the need to provide economically for children that pushes poor women into being prostituted.

Sex trafficking is an extreme example that has been difficult to express in words and is thus rendered unthinkable and unspeakable. For many reasons, women and children as separate subjects do not generally have favored status worldwide and are at risk of losing their psychic reality. Sex trafficking is an extreme illustration of the spectrum of unthinkable and unspeakable experiences in which women can find themselves. As Sister Doherty, a Catholic nun, exclaimed at a United Nations conference, "In ten years, there wasn't one girl or young woman I could stop from getting on that train or bus or plane because they were promised something. But I knew they were being trafficked." It is precisely in a culture where thinking is closed that those involved in sex trafficking live. In a closed-minded culture there is no room for thinking about the reality of otherness. The inability to think about the condition of the victim and the procurers of sex trafficking confirms that they have no history or existence. It is treated as such a hopeless problem that there can be no creative ideas about it. Rather, there is the conclusion that nothing will change the practice of commercial sex resulting in sexual slavery. Despite reactions to the horror of slavery, there may be underlying support of the practice. However, on closer inspection, it is an abject and ignominious condition of culture and the humans involved do not deserve to be relegated to virtual obscurity, especially when one becomes aware of how often it is present and how it is a reflection of our history, legacy, and culture. The larger culture in which sex trafficking prevails is then relegated in the same way. The current and long held beliefs about children as women should be understood as a reflection of sex trafficking. These beliefs mimic the mental and physical state of all the parties involved in sex trafficking as well as the general culture. Psychoanalysts do not practice in a vacuum; everything that is brought to analysis is not merely fantasy. It is important that psychoanalysts do their clinical work with the knowledge of real life events. The broad range of sex trafficking requires an interdisciplinary approach that goes beyond the boundaries of psychoanalytic theory. There are many governmental and nongovernmental organizations that work to combat sex trafficking. APNE International in India has a campaign, "The Last Girl":

"The Last Girl" is the thirteen-year-old in a brothel or the fifteen-year-old standing at a street corner. She is poor, female, and young. Her intersecting inequalities cut off her access to food, clothing, shelter, education and even legal protection. She is the most vulnerable of all human beings to sexual exploitation, and traffickers prey on her vulnerabilities to recruit and pimp her. Each year, 1.4 million girls are sold into sex trafficking. They ask the United Nations to ensure that by 2030, no more girls will be exploited or sold into sex trafficking. (apneaap.org)

Chapter Seven

The Underbelly of Our Culture (and of Psychoanalysis)

John Frank

In his essay titled "Psychoanalysis and Culture: Freud, Erikson, and Bion," Akhtar (2013) suggests that Erikson initiated a perspective that would later come to be known as "anthropological psychoanalysis." Erikson replaced the "classical" epigenetic sequence of the unfolding instincts by a multifactorial perspective that took note of ego capacities, social tasks, and assimilation of group aspirations. He emphasized that the family, school, workplace, and society-at-large are crucial social contexts that contribute significantly to the psychic development of self-esteem and identity formation. Having read and sensed the importance of Erikson's (1950) *Childhood and Society* in college, I was disappointed to learn as a psychoanalytic candidate at my own training center that his major ideas about "cultural influences" were ignored as significant developmental forces in the psychic life of patients. Culture was seen primarily as a product of internal mental conflict rather than as an independent group of realities in their own right.

An esteemed analytic teacher once warned that the "interpersonalists" and "environmentalists" could be a threat to the "pure" culture of psychoanalysis. Here was a powerful psychoanalytic claim, and ego-ideal of purity and "exclusion" from historical, ethnic, and social realities—which had a strong influence on me personally as well as on generations of young analysts. How is it that such a claim was met with little objection or resistance. Perhaps any curiosity about the underlying assumptions behind such ideas was overridden by the promise of belonging to an exclusive culture with its own rituals and benefits for the select few who became annointed as representatives and eventual keepers of this heritage.

This sort of orientation left many questions unanswered. Why were there so few African American candidates, psychotherapy students, or fellows in our training programs? Why was our psychoanalytic center decorated entirely in arts and photographs from the nineteenth and early twentieth century—representing mostly the history and crafts of white American Protestants rather than that of Native Americans or immigrants, who also made up increasing segments of our population? This center had recently moved into a historic 1810 "captain's home" located in the biggest urban park in the country, surrounded by diverse neighborhoods who we neither served nor who were able to use our expertise; we were blind to the diversity in our back yard. Why was our curriculum so long dominated by a "one-person" Oedipal psychology handed down by Freud's followers? And why did it take decades for the psychoanalytic establishment to catch up with other mental health organizations and our culture at large in examining the hurtful role we played in scapegoating homosexuality as gender deviance and in prohibiting gay applicants from gaining admissions to our institutes and centers? Why did it take so long for the problems of sexual boundary violations in analytic training institutes and in clinical practice to be aired with constructive dialogue where remedies could be sought and implemented?

VIVIAN PENDER'S CONTRIBUTION

Dr. Pender's contribution (chapter 6 of this book) would never have made it to a psychiatric medical school symposium when I trained in the 1970s. It is both too "socially real" and too taboo—part of the "unthinkable and unspeakable" underbelly of our culture. But "sex trafficking," Pender tells us, is "an extreme illustration of the spectrum of unthinkable and unspeakable experiences" (p. 23) women and children endure; a spectrum including commercial sex, pornography, domestic abuse, sexual harassment, prejudice toward differences, and the inequalities of poverty, education, child protection systems, and access to health care.

My first comments will be about the child victim, usually female, then the trafficker and buyer, usually male. I will end with comments about how our culture's difficulties in discussing its underbelly might be related to a similar problem in discussing our psychoanalytic culture.

Pender's discussion of child trafficking victims reminded me of a young-adult book written by my niece, Emily, under the name of E. R. Frank, called *Dime* (2015), about teen age trafficking and prostitution. In addition to being a novelist, Emily is a social worker who interviewed and worked with many young people about whom she subsequently wrote. Here is a vignette from *Dime*—maybe similar to the thirteen-year-old "Last Girl" at the end of Pender's chapter. Emily's description of Dime's first meeting with her pimp captures an important piece of Dr. Pender's trafficking culture.

A LITERARY EXTRACT

Thirteen year old Dime is in the foster care system. "There are four females living in a 'stable' in Newark, New Jersey. They have a 'Daddy' and a clean place to sleep and food and clothes. You could say they are being taken care of real nice. Or you could say the secrets they are keeping are like poison eating their souls from the inside out."

Dime has just been kicked out "into the freezing cold" by Janelle, her alcoholic foster mother. The oldest of the 4 in Janelle's home, Dime had come from a group home and had lived with Janelle over three years—the longest of the four girls. Dime had learned that foster mothers don't like you when you get older and Janelle had gone from being not nice to Dime to being nasty. Also, Janelle had told Dime she would get money from welfare for sheets and a blanket which Dime needed because she was skinny and got cold fast. But that never happened. Now Dime sat at a bus stop with no coat in the cold for hours until LA, a girl she had never met before, came over to her and suggested Dime come home with her to meet her boyfriend where they had heat and food.

LA introduces Dime to her boyfriend. "He was tall and dark and smiled at me. 'Hello, Beautiful.' Nobody ever called me beautiful in my entire life. I was so surprised it took me a minute. 'Get this girl some hot food,' he told LA. 'Sit down, Dime,' he told me. 'Make yourself at home.' He pointed to the black leather couch. He put his feet up on the glass coffee table. He was wearing soft-skinned slippers. 'LA been telling me about you saying you in a bad situation where you been staying.' I shrugged."

"'When I talk to you,' he said softly, 'you got to answer me.' I stayed quiet. He slid his slippers off the table, leaned forward and put his hands on my cheeks almost like he was going to kiss me. And also like he was a little bit angry. I was scared of him being angry, but at the same time his hands felt so good and his eyes felt so good. I didn't want him to let me go.

'You understand?' he asked. I started to nod but his hands got just a little bit firmer on my cheeks. They were so big. And warm. I wanted them to stay on my face forever. 'Yes,' I said. 'I understand.' I didn't want to disappoint him. He was looking at me like he saw me. Like he really wanted to hear my voice. Like I mattered. LA brought the soup to the coffee table and set it down in front of me. He let go of my face. I wanted to ask him to put his hands back. But instead, I picked up the spoon and ate. He watched. Only I didn't feel watched; I felt *seen*. 'She going to be good,' he said to LA. I didn't know what he meant. 'You did good.' LA beamed. She looked like a little girl when she beamed like that. I only ever saw her light up with him."

Risks to Dime's psychological well-being include her unstable home life, her caretaker's poverty, rejecting behavior, ignorance of child development, and alcohol abuse. Dime's intense hunger for food, warmth, affection, and love make her highly susceptible to trafficking. "Nobody every called me beautiful in my entire life" is Dime's honest but naive response to Daddy's flattery. Sly fox Daddy (covered in sheep's skin) orders her hot food, tells her to make herself at home, and balances pseudo-empathy with firm expectations. Dime shows caution and fear, but her object hunger—longing for physical affection and caring—are quickly activated by Daddy: "His hands felt so good and his eyes felt so good, I didn't want him to let me go."

In her fantasies, we might imagine Dime substituting Sly-fox Daddy for her absent mother. We never hear about Dime's mother. She could be literally dead or her "dead mother" in Green"s (1980) terminology; this referred to a female parent who was physically alive but psychically dead and preoccupied with her own emotional wounds and unmet needs. Dime's response to Daddy's gaze and touch remind us of Dime's specific early-life deprivations of caretakers able to provide a safe, consistent, and loving human environment. Dime's emotional need for a secure attachment is as basic as her physical needs for nourishment, warmth, and protective safety. Absent of recognition of her own mental state reflected back to her by loving adults, Dime's default self-representation is the caregiver's distorted and barren picture of her, without her own intentional states and agency. We see the Stockholm Syndrome at play in Dime's merger with Daddy, now experienced as the savior parent surrogate (Fonagy and Target 1998). A few chapters later, with further guile and flattery, and with the appearance of mutual consent, Dime loses her virginity to Daddy—the first step in Dime becoming a prostituted person.

The euphemism "Daddy" for "pimp" speaks to the ironic willingness of this culture to deny the rage against such men where a term of ordinary endearment covers the horror of their "double think" or "soul murder" (Shengold, 1989). The denial of murderous rage in the victim also allows the preservation of the internal fantasied protective other who is always needed to prevent a form of primitive annihilation anxiety. For the more fortunate among us, the word *daddy* connotes love, strength, the representation of reality, and the safety of clear generational and sexual boundaries.

Moving to the male trafficker and buyer, Dr. Pender's brief vignettes of Jack, a trafficker, and Ronald, a buyer, have in common the difficult relationships with hypercritical controlling mothers negatively affecting both their masculine self-image and their capacity for intimacy with women. Extrapolating from incest relationships, Pender suggests that men who are sex traffickers, buyers, and perpetrators of incest feel ownership toward, and lack of differentiation from their child victims. In their own childhoods, these men never developed a sense of agency and self-hood from a healthy mother-child matrix. Instead, they grew up silenced as voiceless non-people. Khan's (1963) notion of "cumulative trauma" is also relevant here where mother's role as a protective shield over the course of a child's development is breached, leaving the child to try and defend against his continued need for mother to support his immature and unstable ego functions.

Fischer (1991) has written similarly about abusive men whose low self-esteem, poorly developed identity, and lack of empathy for the child's immaturity and dependency relates to their having been emotionally deprived themselves. During incestuous sexual union, the parent with a history of early deprivation can feel triumphant over their own unconscious feelings of helplessness and rage. Fischer believes that in incest, "father's healthy role as modulator of aggression and provider of nurturance" (p. 48) is significantly absent.

Pender's (2017) edited book, *The Status of Women Violence, Identity, and Activism,* integrates a psychoanalytic, historical and cultural perspective. In the chapter, "Machismo and the Limits of Male Heterosexuality," Tylim (2017), an analyst from Argentina, looks at his South American masculine heritage. He reviews the atrocities toward and systemic humiliation of indigenous natives in large portions of Meso and South America by the European conquistadors beginning in the fifteenth century; native language, customs, and religion were brutally attacked destroying the soul of Latin America's ancient civilizations. Fusing the crown, cross, and sword, such "colonization" relied on a binary idealization of masculinity and devaluation of woman, supported by a punitive male-dominated church and government. The Inquisition, a court run exclusively by men, affirmed the ruling male-centered institutions. It wasn't just the land that was colonized—it was the subjectivity of its inhabitants that was silenced into nonexistence. Tylim believes the legacy of colonization with its "cultural values and ideologies" has been passed down for generations to our time and exists today in many forms in Latin American and beyond. The macho battlefield is played out aggressively in the political world and with male brutal force at home. Macho men on top of the hierarchy exercise their privilege and ignore, use, abuse, or control those under them.

In our long held patriarchal tradition with its power differentials, men dominate the highest levels of society's institutions; corporations, board rooms, universities, and psychoanalytic institutes where gender subjugation—although often more subtle than in the past—still thrives. More about psychoanalytic institutes later.

How to understand *machismo*? Tylim asks. It is a derivative of macho and an extreme stereotyped hypermasculinity. One meaning is a perverse attempt to ward off the threat of castration anxiety—like those animal species who make themselves look much bigger and more threatening than they really are. Behavioral defenses protect against vulnerability, softness, passive longings, domesticity, and caretaking impulses. Tylim's macho man hates his binary feminine side. These unacceptable traits are projected onto the "other" as is the wish to depend on an all powerful but resented mother figure of childhood or her substitute. Tylim ends his chapter with the optimistic suggestion that many contemporary males are now aware of how much is lost in holding onto old masculine gender constructions and performances. In what he calls a "liberating movement," these men are willing to abandon such masculine stereotypes in the hopes that they can be more open to their warded off and walled off "feminine" side.

THE CULTURE AT LARGE

Pender too points to the "implicit cultural acceptance" of this underbelly-transmitted from one generation to the next in what appears to be a closed system resistant to change. As a fourteen-year-old visiting my family in Florida in the 1950s, I was startled by the overt racial discrimination I saw in public train stations, in buses, and in local customs. When I tried to understand what I saw there by asking my college-educated aunt about it, she told me that colored people were really quite satisfied with the current arrangements because they were like small children getting taken care of and getting their needs met. This was her attempt to transmit her cultural acceptance of the status quo to me. Looking back sixty years, my aunt may have been satisfied at being taken care of and getting her needs met but not the other way around. In sex trafficking, buyers and traffickers initiate and sustain these activities. Victims are frequently silently resigned and unable to imagine successful liberation.

If we were to ask the 108 million people (one third of our population) who watch the Super Bowl what they think of the fact that this great American moment of mass market and cultural cohesion draws the most sex trafficking, including girls transported there in buses, we might get three responses. The vast majority would say they did not know about it. The pimps and buyers would justify their behavior on economic, or biological naturalness/necessity grounds, and the victims might remain silent. But just as the effects of football injuries on players future lives is entering our culture's awareness, so is the scale of human trafficking. There are now public advertisements at many sporting events warning of the danger of trafficking (Harris, 2017).

While sex trafficking and its associated cultural demons are still our cultural underbelly, we now seeing the first wide spread recognition of a piece of this underbelly in the #MeToo and Time's Up movements. Beginning in the entertainment industry and taking hold in all three branches of government, universities, groups of farm workers, housekeepers, waitresses, domestics, and health aides, widespread protests are ongoing against our sexual exploitation culture. This dramatic changes in response to sexual harassment and assault depicted in our media has been described by some as a tsunami or earthquake. Will the systemic power imbalances keeping women underrepresented continue to be addressed and gain momentum with demands for accountability and consequences for sexual misconduct? And if true change is in the offing will it extend to those women and children whose means and voice have been the least and quietest amongst us?

A few last thoughts about our culture's values through the eyes of two well known non-analysts. Pinker (2011), in his book *The Better Angels of Our Nature*, suggests that violence has declined—less war and improved treatment of children—from a greater capacity for empathy (we feel the pain of others), better self-control, and a stronger moral sense governing people's interactions. Violence can increase on the other hand "when the norms are tribal, authoritarian, or puritanical." Albright (2018), in a recent *New York Times* op ed page, titled "Will We Stop Trump Before It's Too Late?" writes, "Instead of mobilizing international coalitions to take on world problems, he touts the doctrine of 'every nation for itself.' Mr Trump with his scorn for democracy's building blocks has strengthened the hands of dictators." She warns against a "there's nothing to be done" approach to his authoritarian presidency.

The president of the United States—maybe the most powerful man in the world—is a magnet for our complex transference feelings (to father) as individuals and groups: men, women, children, Democrats, Republicans, NRA members, and immigrants. While Trump embraces conservative family values, and signed a bill giving federal and state prosecutors the power to pursue websites hosting sex-trafficking ads, he is disdainful toward women, takes pride in what he can get away, and projects an aggressive masculinity as the leader of the nation and of the free world. What messages does President Trump give about "The Culture of Sex Trafficking"?

SOME FINAL THOUGHTS

Pender has helped us to think and speak in ways that were unimaginable forty years ago. What was "culturally unconscious" is—in bits and pieces—with the help of social media—becoming conscious in the form of new conversations and constructive action. While she reminds committed psychoanalysts that we do not practice in a vacuum and that what is brought to us in the clinical setting is more than fantasy, the fantasy/reality issue as it bares on our cultural discussion is once again receiving serious attention within mainstream psychoanalysis.

For decades, analysts misused the ideas of the Oedipus complex to explain homosexuality (Chodorow, 2002; Dresher, 2008) and downplayed the enormous role parents' own early experiences and personal ghosts have in their children's emotional and behavioral lives (Ferenczi, 1933). Such misuse of Oedipus left a theoretical gap in our understanding of gender, sexuality, their normal variations, and the limitations of our treatments. This has been a humbling experience for many of us.

Simon (1992) became interested in the area of actual trauma, especially incest and sexual contact between patient and therapist. He had been supervising cases of patients who had been sexually abused by therapists and analysts, and connected these experiences with some of the emergent findings on the sequelae of childhood sexual abuse. There seemed to be similar mechanisms of defense involved in the patients abused by therapists and patients abused by parents—denial, rage, protection of the guilty perpetrator, extreme guilt and shame, some form of dissociation, or at the least a fluctuating disbelief in what had actually happened . . . mechanisms of defense among therapists, including analysts, involved disavowal of the actuality of these events. (It doesn't happen—the women make it up; if it does happen, the women are seductive; it doesn't happen with well-trained therapists, and certainly not analysts; it only happens with wild therapists, pastoral counselors, fraudulently licensed people.) Simon pointed out that these mechanisms of disavowal seen in therapists were similar to those that operated in relation to incest.

Analysts must live with their own incomplete Oedipal resolutions and lingering biases (Dimen 2014), a reminder of the continuing work we all need to do on ourselves. Confronting the realities of gross sexual abuse and violence toward children (Kempe, Silverman, and Steele, 1962) as well as more subtle parental failures of attunement and attachment Fonagy (2001) has led to a reevaluation of Oedipal and pre-Oedipal paradigms in our educational programs. Pender mentions Young-Bruehl's (2012) contribution to failures of adults to respect the rights of children in her coining the term, "childism" to cover an array of predjudices and other motivations which undermine or abort the healthy development of childhood.

Confronting the realities of analyst sexual boundary violations (Gabbard, 2016) has awakened analysts' greater accountability to their patients and their colleagues and the need for consultation and on going courses in ethics and counter-transference enactments. The fact is that many in the psychoanalytic community are now acknowledging the enormous role of social-historical turmoil, ethnic, racial, economic and religious differences and the realities of Society that Erikson wrote about in the 1950s and 1960s. Their contributions are not only about cultural phenomena in society at large but include sustained looks at ourselves as groups of analysts in our own institutions with our various subcultures, rivalries, power structures, and discriminations. Ideally this newer viewpoint can develop without our having to give up basic analytic principles such as the focus on unconscious conflict in psychic live, child development, transference-countertranseference, and reflective functioning. We have seen in today's Mahler symposium the transition in our psychoanalytic history from Freud's discoveries of childhood sexuality with its emphasis on the conscious and unconscious agency of the child to considerations of the traumatic victumization of the child in *The Rape of Childhood.*

While the underbelly of our culture and of our psychoanalytic field have led some to feel frustrated at the slow pace of change, Pender has mentioned several examples of small but significant breakthroughs; the 2000 Palermo Protocols and Trafficking Victims Protection Act, (Pender, 2017) Tylim's "liberating moments," where men examine themselves and become more open to their feminine side, and the signs at sporting events warning about trafficking. I have also mentioned the examples of Madeleine Albright's inspiration against apathy and Steven Pinker's better angels of our nature. Martin Luther King Jr. (1958) is known for saying, "The arc of the moral universe is long but ends in justice" (p. 14).

Chapter Eight

Shattered Children

A Concluding Commentary

Ann G. Smolen

The three main chapters contained in this book (chapters 2, 4, and 6, by Thomas Barrett, Calvin Colarusso, and Vivian Pender, respectively) describe a myriad of sexual abuses against children. Whether the abuser was a family member, teacher, stranger, or pimp, the child's innocence was destroyed, and his or her sense of self was shattered. Some children who were lucky enough to obtain good-enough therapy began to heal and were able to make their way in the world. Not all children thus affected are so fortunate. They are psychically deadened and unable to trust others. They live in a dissociated state often supported by drug addiction. In order to understand the complexities of child sexual abuse, I will not only review the contributions of Drs. Barrett, Colarusso, and Pender, I will also place them in the context of historically evolving psychoanalytic theory in this realm.

EARLY THEORY

In one of his etiological hypotheses, Freud (1895, 1896) proposed that all neuroses were caused by sexual seduction of children by adults. This could vary from overstimulation, visually and/or verbally, to physical sexual abuse. Freud's "seduction hypothesis" proposed that when a child was over-stimulated sexually (verbally, visually, or physically) by an adult, the result was anxiety and repression. Later, repressed memories were triggered by an event, which led to symptom formation. Freud believed, for example, that all of his hysterical female patients had experienced sexual trauma as children. As a result, their hysterical symptoms symbolized and communicated repressed traumatic sexual memories. Over time, Freud came to doubt his seduction hypothesis and replaced it with a theory of intrapsychic causation. He purported that his hysterical female patients' "memories" of seduction were intrapsychic fantasies, which in turn were remnants of unconscious childhood wishes (Person and Klar, 1994).

This striking change from seduction in reality to intrapsychic childhood fantasies was pivotal in the evolution of psychoanalytic theory and technique. From then on, psychoanalytic ideas became grounded in the study of wishes and fantasies that derive from the unruly and anachronistic unconscious. In other words, exploring unconscious conflicts was the focus of psychoanalytic thinking and practice. Traumatic events in the lives of patients were no longer of consequence, which in turn diminished the significance of reconstructing childhood memories. Until recent years, most American analysts emphasized unconscious mental contents and their transformations as the chief interest of psychoanalysis. The focus has been on how these fantasies impacted reality, but not the other way around. This is undoubtedly a one-person psychology (Person and Klar, 1994). However, Freud (1940) continued to think of actual seduction as one possible cause of adult symptom formation and never gave up entirely on his seduction hypothesis (Blum, 2008).

As psychoanalytic theory evolved, some analysts gave up trying to reconstruct the past and accepted psychoanalysis as a hermeneutic science, while many others took the position that unconscious fantasies are impossible to differentiate from repressed memories. We know that memories are condensed and altered over time and are multiply determined as well as multilayered with meanings. We also understand that prohibited fantasies and real experiences often merge, but that should not preclude addressing the actual trauma.

This reality becomes even more painful when the sexual abuse is perpetrated by the child's parents (Kramer and Akhtar, 1991; Gartner, 1997; Shengold, 1999; Colarusso, 2011). Such an occurrence can fortify the effects of the child's forbidden Oedipal fantasies (Greenacre, 1956). The trauma of incest is devastating and overwhelming, it "is an act of unmodulated aggression against a helpless child" (Fischer, 1991, p. 48). Nothing the child has known can prepare him/her for it and nothing he or she can do can make it go away. He or she is unable to self-protect and the child is left without the protection of another adult. He or she has no one upon whom she can depend for safety and well-being. One of the most destructive outcomes of sexual trauma is the disruption of thinking. This intrusion upon the unconscious and conscious thought processes results in the inability to represent the trauma symbolically. When conscious and unconscious processes are disrupted, "cognitive structure, sign recognition, symbol formation, syntax, discrimination and the availability to use these capacities to formulate and organize language are either absent or are present but ineffectual" (Nachmani, 1995, p. 423). When incest occurs, there is a blurring of boundaries, which informs the child that the environment is unsafe. The child is left vulnerable and defenseless in the face of danger. When the environment is experienced as having caused pain from neglect and abuse, there is a "radical break between trauma and expectation, victims often cannot find categories of thought or words" (Nachmani, 1995, p. 424). Another consequence of such severe boundary violation is that there is a "formidable destruction of the capacity to 'make sense,' to preserve order, to sustain a fundamental sense of the order of relatedness through the use of symbols and language and the trustworthy reliance upon others" (Nachmani, 1995, p. 425). These humiliating, shameful, and pain-ridden violations can cause the cessation of mental growth. In addition to a defect in symbolic thinking, reality testing is also compromised (Kramer, 1991).

When child/parent incest occurs, *betrayal* becomes a trauma in its own right. A child is dependent on a parent for care, love, and safety. When the parent uses the nature of this dependent relationship for sexual exploitation and harm, it undermines the meaning of dependency. "In betrayal, a pseudo-dependency is created by deceit based on trust. Betrayals are traumatic because trust is broken, while the need to depend on others remains" (Nachmani 1995, p. 425). When incest occurs, the child is being deceived, and meanings become confusing. What does it mean to have privacy? How to understand trust? When this terrible betrayal transpires, object-constancy ceases to develop, and the separation-individuation process becomes impaired (Nachmani, 1995).

Another traumatic outcome of the incestuous relationship is the child's not being seen as a separate person. Nachmani (1995) describes this phenomenon as "when people act 'as if' one were absent" (p. 429). The abuser denies that his child has a "self" or a mind of her own. Many victims of father/daughter incest experience feelings of emptiness as if they have no self. Their needs have been ignored and denied. However, the child is trapped and must keep that parent available to avoid annihilation anxiety and total abandonment. Many children make use of dissociation in order to keep the parent "good." The child cannot tolerate the fear of family disintegration, and at times, incest is seen as keeping the family together (Cohler, 1987). Children who are the victims of their parent's unmitigated rage are overwhelmed and rendered helpless by their own feelings of fury. "But this rage must be denied in order to maintain the sense of the good parent" (Fischer 1991, pp. 53). It is also important to note that some semblance of self is sought, "being misrecognized feels so much more secure than being unrecognized and unknown. 'As if' is better than 'no if'" (Nachmani, 1995, p. 430).

When incest occurs early, the separation-individuation process is disturbed and thus "abused children manifest a great vulnerability to separation problems, depression, and splitting of good and bad self and good and bad object" (Kramer, 1991, pp. 4). These children also experience intolerable sexual excitement that becomes unmanageable, tremendous anger, and an overwhelming sense of helplessness and powerlessness. When an abused child reaches adolescence, there is a tendency for masochistic behaviors such as eating disorders and cutting.

BARRETT'S CONTRIBUTION

Thomas Barrett begins by offering us a snapshot of theory of childhood abuse, citing Katan's (1973) paper, "Children Who Were Raped," and Shengold's (1979) groundbreaking work, *Soul Murder*. Barrett concludes this short theoretical introduction by telling us that it is the compulsion to repeat that brings children and adolescents into treatment. He emphasizes that as children who have suffered abuse enter the developmental phase of adolescence, there is an escalation of emotions and impulses, which in turn may cause repressed traumatic memories to resurface. He adds that turning passive into active may turn aggression toward the self, resulting in depression. For Barrett, it is the reactivation of traumatic memories that cause a myriad of symptoms that halt development and bring children and adolescents into our treatment rooms. I would add that development was arrested when the abuse occurred and then repressed. As children enter new developmental phases, the old traumas and conflicts are reactivated and new symptoms develop.

Barrett then takes us on an analytic journey where we, the audience, become observers of his gentle, empathic, and point-on analytic technique, where healing is given the opportunity to begin as he works with Amy, his abused adolescent patient. Barrett tells Amy's story of sexual abuse by her mother's boyfriend's thirteen-year-old son when she was six years old. Amy was able to go to her mother for help and the abuse stopped, but the damage was done. Barrett demonstrates that when Amy became an adolescent, her repressed trauma memories returned in the form of self-destructive behaviors. Barrett supports his analytic work with Amy, referencing once again Katan's paper on sexual abuse of children who stated that one of the most debilitating consequences of childhood sexual abuse is the disturbance of drive fusion causing the child to turn aggression upon the self. He also includes the work of Erna Furman (1956), and the more contemporary writings of Pynoos (1990, 1993), van der Kolk (1987, 1996, 2014), and Liberman and Van Horn (2008), to round out a comprehensive literature review.

Barrett demonstrates his excellent analytic intuition and skill in his work with three-year-old Ben, and four-year-old Joey, both boys who had been sexually molested. Young Ben replayed his sexual abuse through somatic behaviors, making use of his body to help tell his analyst what had happened to him. He defecated during his treatment, which allowed his analyst to speak with him about how scared he was when the bad man touched him, so scared he defecated. Barrett, in a nonintrusive way, put words to Ben's somatic communications. I will not recount the details of these two superb analyses, but instead I will leave the reader with a three questions that arose in my mind by his presentation: (i) How does the analyst get into the mind of an abused child?; (ii) Why do adults abuse children? What is it that overrides morality and trust?; and (iii) Where does the malignant hostility come from when an adult destroys innocence? These quibbles notwithstanding, I was left deeply impressed by Barrett's technical expertise when working with abused children and their parents. His treatment of Amy, Ben, and Joey are a tribute to his nonintrusive, kind, and empathic approach, where he asks permission of his young patient when asking a question or making an interpretation, and he always allows the child to control and direct the treatment.

COLARUSSO'S CONTRIBUTION

It is not unusual for adolescent boys to have crushes on female teachers as well as on "hot mothers" of their friends. These crushes help facilitate the second separation/individuation process as boys mature both psychologically and sexually. Calvin Colarusso has forty years of experience as an expert witness in cases of sexual abuse by adult female teachers with their adolescent students. This work is valuable as there are no references in the psychoanalytic literature to sexual abuse between adult female teachers and their male adolescent students. The three cases presented are not clinical treatments of the abuse victims, but rather detailed histories of their abusive experiences through interviews conducted by Colarusso. He demonstrates how this specific type of sexual abuse by an adult female teacher on her male adolescent student assaulted and derailed the adolescents' psychosocial development. Colarusso makes an excellent case for the damage ensued by the betrayal of the adult/student trust and the disregard of appropriate boundaries.

Jack, the youngest victim, was just thirteen years old when his abuse occurred. Colarusso interviewed both the mother and Jack separately when Jack was just under eighteen years old. It is evident from the history that Jack's life leading up to his abuse was difficult. His parents had never married and his father was in jail. In addition, Jack had already fathered his own child and he, his girlfriend and baby were living with his mother. After his teacher seduced him, Jack was embarrassed and felt great shame that caused him to drink heavily. In addition, he spent three months in juvenile hall for breaking and entering when he was fifteen years old. Colarusso states that

Jack was robbed of any chance of having a carefree adolescence. He feels the abuse directly caused regression in Jack's ability to learn, as well as inhibiting his emotional and sexual development. While, I agree with Colarusso's understanding of Jack's arrested development, I do feel Jack was a high-risk child to begin with, which may have made him more vulnerable to seduction by the predatory teacher than a child in a healthier environment.

Andrew was sixteen years old when his sexual abuse by his teacher took place. Colarusso interviewed the parents twice and met with Andrew three times. Unlike Jack, Andrew grew up in an intact middle-class family. After Andrew's sexual encounters with his teacher, he developed insomnia often staying up all night. He had nightmares and described himself as feeling paranoid. Colarusso aptly stated that Andrew's case is a perfect example of how a sexual relationship between an adolescent boy and his teacher can turn into an actual "nightmare." Andrew was diagnosed with major depression as well as PTSD. Andrew was luckier than Jack, as he was referred to a child analyst and received psychotherapy until he was able to go away to college.

The third and last case presented is Elijah who was fifteen years old when he became sexually involved with his teacher. Colarusso met with the mother once and met twice with Elijah. Elijah's parents were never married and his father was sporadically involved with his son. The family lived in public housing. Elijah reacted to his abuse very differently than Jack and Andrew did. Elijah proclaimed love for his teacher and hoped one day to be with her. Colarusso points out that the sexual abuse undermined Elijah's adolescent development; as with Jack, Elijah was born into poverty without the best opportunities to reach his potential.

Colarusso ends his chapter with a rich and thoughtful explanation of the differences in the three cases and how they progressed. He concludes that the "effects of childhood and adolescent sexual abuse are ongoing and life-long and affect not only the victims, but family members as well" (p. 75).

PENDER'S CONTRIBUTION

Vivian Pender begins her sobering presentation by educating her audience as to the definition of sex trafficking: "The buying and selling of persons for the purpose of sexual exploitation; the act of harboring, recruiting, or transporting a person by means of force, fraud, or coercion for the purpose of sexual exploitation." She then stuns her audience by telling us that it was not until 2000 that the Palermo Protocol, an international treaty to "Prevent, Suppress and Punish Trafficking in Persons Especially Women and Children" became law. Sex trafficking is ubiquitous. It takes up residence in nail salons, truck stops, hotels, professional conferences, fracking sites, and the Super Bowl. The buyers come from all socioeconomic strata, from the uneducated to our most prominent citizens and professionals. Pender states what is undeniable: sexual enslavement of vulnerable persons is unthinkable and unspeakable yet it is everywhere all over the world and has been in existence since the beginning of civilization. Pender continues to educate her audience as she describes the various forms of sex trafficking such as illegal child marriage and legalized brothels. Most recently, sex trafficking also afflicts refugee and migrant camps. Trafficking does not require movement. It is pervasive in every city and happens to those who are most vulnerable. Trafficking was even happening on Craigslist and backpage.com until this year, when laws were passed to ban it from these internet sites.

Pender asks the questions: What is it in our culture that allows sexual exploitation of children to exist? What is the role of culture in sex trafficking? She attempts to answer these unfathomable questions by supplying important facts such as the male perspective dominates sex trafficking and is driven by the desire for sexual services. There are twenty-one million individuals who are victims of sex trafficking. Five and a half million of these are children. Within the United States, 80 percent are U.S. citizens. Pender states that while boys are trafficked, the majority are girls and the majority of buyers are men. She points to power as being the key factor as the victims are often children who are born into poverty, lack education, and are displaced refugees due to conflict in their native countries. The average age is twelve and the child may service buyers (strange men) as many as fifty times per night. Pender describes that the children are often psychotic with fragmented selves. Their only defense is to become dissociated.

There has been some forward movement whereas the vulnerable victims are no longer treated as criminals but instead are offered treatment. The criminals are the sellers and the buyers. However, this is not a panacea as Pender warns that these fragmented children do not trust anyone and have no psychological safe space. In their minds, everyone is untrustworthy. Physicians in urgent care units and emergency rooms now include the following questions in an effort to identify sex trafficked victims and their buyers: (i) Have you ever been forced to engage in sex?; and (ii) Have you ever paid for sex? Pender leaves us with the notion that within the sex trafficking world, there is a cultural psychodynamic of helplessness is infused with sadism. Her contribution is indeed a sobering message that needs more attention.

I would like to commend Pender for undertaking such heart-wrenching work, making use of psychoanalytic thinking in her understanding of, and her interactions with these traumatized young women/children. Her chapter clearly tells us that a *mental crime* is occurring when children are sexually exploited and abused. Pender makes use of Shengold's (1979, 1989, 1999) term "soul murder." I will expand on this line of thought. Soul murder is the malicious abuse and neglect of children by adults. When a child is traumatized in this way, her consequent emotional development is profoundly negatively affected and severely compromised. The abuses suffered by trafficked children and then reenacted at the hands of the pimp have destroyed their childhood innocence that will never be recovered. These children become deadened; their fragile developing selves have been murdered. I imagine that all of the children who succumb to the seduction and coercion of the pimp have been abused (mostly sexual abuse) by either a family member or a *friend* of the family. When a relatively helpless child is physically and/or sexually abused, she or he becomes extremely over stimulated, which in turn, evokes traumatic anxiety and rage. When the child's abuse comes in the form of neglect, which I suspect these children also experienced, this over stimulation may result in rage and intense sexual longing. I speculate that the children Pender writes about have encountered multiple abuses throughout their young lives.

CONCLUSION

Every child deserves, needs, and expects "good-enough" parenting. Children cannot survive without parents and they need to believe that the adults will protect them and keep them safe. Abused children have no choice but to look for rescue by the same person who committed the abuse. This is mind-splitting and causes sadomasochistic impulses such as perverse sexual excitement and murderous wishes. When this happens, the child must guard against these traumatic feelings by developing massive defenses, which include dissociation, again, a splitting of the mind. These children must defend against the rage they felt toward the abusing parent/pimp so they become dead inside, what Shengold (1989) calls "emotional zombies," or they cannot control their impulses and become drug addicts. Their pimps also feed them drugs. That is why victimized children can turn tricks one minute and the next minute seem unaffected the next. Abused children grip tightly to whatever benevolent parenting exists and cling to the delusion that their parents are loving and caring. This is actually one of the most destructive effects of child abuse: the need to hold onto the abusing parent or parental figure. Children must deny what has taken place as if it did not happen.

Clearly all children who are physically and sexually abused are also emotionally neglected. The adult does not care about them or see them as separate individuals with feelings and thoughts, and with a mind of their own. The children that Pender describes most probably did not have parents who were able to mentalize. The capacity to mentalize is an important developmental accomplishment. When a child develops this reflective ability, she then has a sense of her own mind as separate from the mind of the other. When the parent is able to mentalize, the child feels understood, thought about, and reflected upon. The parent with reflective capacities can hold onto the mind of her child, which in turn, promotes in the child a developing sense of herself as a separate person with her own thoughts and feelings. I speculate that the parents of trafficked children carried their own traumatic burdens that have been transmitted unconsciously to their children. A parent who is consumed by her own unprocessed abuses cannot view her child with a clear mind, especially when the child is experiencing overwhelming affects such as despair and/or fear.

It is here that I want to speak about Silverman's (2015) concept of the "colonized mind," which occurs when the parent's fears and traumatic experiences are projected into the developing mind of the child. "The colonizer seeks to own and control in the unconscious hope of preventing the colonized from developing an independent and separate identity" (p. 54). Silverman clarifies that mentalizing is about making space in order to create room for thought and reflection. It is about co-creating together in a relationship. Colonizing, on the other hand, destroys space and invades the mind of the other not allowing the child to think. To colonize another's mind is to intrude and destroy. It seems obvious, that the pimps are stand-ins for the original parental figures. I imagine that the pimps carry out their own abusive histories that are reenacted on young girls as they colonize their minds. These children do not run away from their captors because they have nowhere to go, but they also have few coping mechanisms; they are virtually paralyzed and unable to help themselves.

Drs. Barrett, Colarusso, and Pender demonstrate the devastating effect that sexual abuse (and all abuse) has on the psychological development of children. We certainly see this reenacted between trafficked children and their pimp. He abuses them and they cannot leave him, they cling to him hoping to be cared for and loved. Abused children have never really been loved. Instead, their love has been betrayed, which leaves the child in a state of tormented longing. There is a compulsion to repeat past traumatic experiences, a need to reenact the unforgettable agony as both victim and persecutor. Freud (1920) taught us that within this compulsion to repeat, there is a wish for past traumatic experiences to be reversed, unfortunately, in most cases, this fails. An example of this is when the abused child ages and now, as a thirty-year old woman, she is no longer the desired prize by the buyer, she becomes the enforcer, reenacting past trauma over and over as both victim and abuser.

The children who have shared their stories with Drs. Barrett, Colarusso, and Pender have been seduced and betrayed by the act of seduction, which can have an overwhelming destructive effect on a child's intrapsychic stability and development. If the original seduction and abuse occurred during the Oedipal phase when the little girl is "in love" with her father and wishes to steal him away from the mother, her Oedipal fantasies are reinforced by a reality experience, the resulting disorganizing effect is immense. The child may experience conscious and unconscious rage toward her seducer as well as feelings of guilt. The defense of repression is commonly induced, which protects the child from the incestuous meaning of the seductive behavior. In addition, an unconscious desire and need for punishment will arise.

How do we reach these shattered and fragmented children? How can we understand how their minds work? How can we as therapists gain their trust? How do those who have suffered soul murder learn to live again? Shengold (1989) tells us that only love can restore the soul. Soul murder leaves in its wake the inability to care about and love others, which includes the self. In psychoanalytic psychotherapy and psychoanalysis, we depend on our patient's capacity to love. I would speculate that the girls Pender writes about would experience feeling love for the benevolent therapist as dangerous. The suffering these children have endured is deeply buried, covered over by anger and hate, which are much easier emotions to tolerate. It is important to remember that the abusing parent or pimp has become a part of the abused child's identity. If she allows herself to love her therapist, she risks losing a part of herself, herself as victim and self as persecutor.

If undertaken, this therapeutic journey will be challenging and arduous. The therapist must be able to tolerate long periods of rage and must be on the lookout for the child's compulsion to repeat her traumatic history with the therapist. I imagine that sadomasochistic enactments would occur and it is important to resist getting entwined in these interactions. The child must be able to ask the question, "Is there life without my abuser?" She will need to learn to admit that she cannot and does not want to let go of her abusing parental figure and she must be able to tolerate her murderous rage toward her therapist. Most of all, she needs to admit that she lives in hell and that her demons are real. If she can do this, change can occur, and healing can begin. This is not a quick fix and will take a very long time, but if accomplished, the abused girl may begin to think of herself as a person, retrieve the ability to love and the capacity to love that she was born with that was tragically taken from her when her soul was murdered.

All of the professionals who work with these children must employ patience and must find that place of empathy in their hearts looking past the murderous rage and contemptuous behaviors to see the helpless abused little children they once were. The ultimate goal is for those professionals working with these children to think of gently guiding them toward being able to tolerate loving and being loved. It would be an enormous therapeutic challenge to aid these children in the ability to once again and maybe for the first time, care about themselves.

References

Abraham, K. (1907). The experiencing of sexual traumas as a form of sexual activity. In: *Selected Papers of Karl Abraham*, pp. 47–63. London: Hogarth Press, 1927.

Abrams, S. (1978). The teaching and learning of psychoanalytic developmental psychology. *Journal of the American Psychoanalytic Association* 26: 387–406.

Ahbel-Rappe, K. (2006). "I no longer believe": Did Freud abandon the seduction theory? *Journal of the American Psychoanalytic Association* 54: 171–199.

Ahmed, A.G. (2014). Dysfunctional anger and sexual violence. *Psychiatric Clinics of North America,* 37(2): 231–238.

Akhtar, S. (2009). *Comprehensive Dictionary Of Psychoanalysis*. London: Karnac.

Akhtar, S. (2013) Psychoanalysis and culture: Freud, Erikson, and beyond. In: *Psychoanalysis in Asia: China, India, Japan, South Korea, Taiwan*, eds. A. Gerlach, M.T. Savio Hooke, and S. Varin, pp. 19–41. London: Karnac Books.

Albright, M. (2018) Will we stop Trump before it's too late? *New York Times*, Op Ed, 4/8/2018.

Albright, M. (2018) *Fascism: A Warning*. New York: Harper Collins

Allen, C. (1991). *Women and Men who Sexually Abuse Children: A Comparative Analysis.* Orwell, VT: Safer Society Press.

Ammerman, R., Kolko, D., Kirisci, L., Blackson, T., and Dawes, M. (1999). Child abuse potential in parents with histories of substance abuse disorder. *Child Abuse and Neglect* 23: 1225–1238.

Andersen, R.A., Bancroft, J., and Wu F.C.W. (1992). The effects of exogenous testosterone on sexuality and mood of normal men. *Journal of Clinical Endocrinology and Metabolism* 75: 1503–1507.

Apne Aap International. The petition. http://apneaap.org/ Accessed March 20, 2018.

Apprey, M. (1991). Psychical transformations by a child of incest. In: *The Trauma of Transgression: Psychotherapy of Incest Victims*, eds. S. Kramer and S. Akhtar, pp. 115–147. Northvale, NJ: Jason Aronson.

Auerhahn, N.C., and Laub, D. (1987). Play and playfulness in Holocaust survivors. *The Psychoanalytic Study of the Child* 42: 45–58.

Ávila, A., and Domínguez, R. (2014). Dreams and change processes in an ex-prostitute under relational psychoanalytic psychotherapy: Ferenczian and relational views. *International Forum of Psychoanalysis* 23: 23–29.

Balsam, R.H. (1996). The pregnant mother and the body image of the daughter. *Journal of the American Psychoanalytic Association* 44S: 401–427.

Bancroft, J. (2012). The behavioral correlates of testosterone. In: *Testosterone: Action, Deficiency, Substitution,* eds. E. Nieschlag, H.M. Behre, and S. Nieschlag, pp. 87–122. Cambridge, UK: Cambridge University Press.
Barton, R., and Whitehead, J. (1969). The gaslight phenomenon. *Lancet* 1: 1258–1260.
Begle, A.M., Dumas, J.E., and Hanson, R.F. (2010). Predicting child abuse potential: An empirical investigation of two theoretical frameworks. *Journal of Clinical Child and Adolescent Psychology* 39: 208–219.
Bennett, J. (2017) The click moment: The Weinstein scandal unleashed a tsunami. *New York Times*, 11/5/2017.
Bennett-Murphy, L.M. (2012). Haunted: Treatment of a child survivor of human trafficking. *Journal of Infant Child Adolescent Psychotherapy* 11: 133–148.
Besinger, B., Garland, A., Litrownik, A., and Landsverk, J. (1999). Caregiver substance abuse among maltreated children placed in out-of-home care. *Child Welfare* 78: 221–239.
Bigras, J. (1990). Psychoanalysis as incestuous repetition: Some technical considerations. In: *Adult Analysis and Childhood Sexual Abuse*, ed. H. Levine, pp. 173–196. Hillsdale, NJ: Analytic Press.
Birch, P. (2015). *Why Men Buy Sex: Examining Sex Worker Clients.* London: Routledge.
Blos, P. (1967). The second individuation process in adolescence. *Psychoanalytic Study of the Child* 22: 162–186.
Blos, P. (1979). *The Adolescent Passage.* New York: International Universities Press.
Blum, H.P. (2008). A further excavation of seduction, seduction trauma, and the seduction theory. *Psychoanalytic Study of the Child* 63: 254–269.
Bohm, B., Zollner, H., Fegert, J.M., and Liebhardt, H. (2014) Child sexual abuse in the context of the Roman Catholic Church: A review of literature from 1981–2013. *Journal of Child Sexual Abuse* 23: 635–656.
Brenner, I. (1994). The dissociative character: A reconsideration of "multiple personality." *Journal of the American Psychoanalytic Association* 42: 819–846.
Brenner, I. (1996). On trauma, perversion, and "multiple personality." Journal of the American Psychoanalytic Association 44: 785–814.
Brenner, I. (2001). *Dissociation of Trauma: Theory, Phenomenology, and Technique*. Madison, CT: International Universities Press.
Brenneis, C.B. (1994). Belief and suggestion in the recovery of memories of childhood sexual abuse. *Journal of the American Psychoanalytic Association* 42: 1027–1053.
Brothers, D. (2014). "Crimes against humanity" and the societal context of trauma: Discussion of "A Sense of 'Being Human' and Twinship Experience" by Koichi Togashi. *International Journal of Psychoanalytic Self Psychology* 9: 282–288.
Bruck, M., and Ceci, S.J. (1999). The suggestibility of children's memory. *Annual Review of Psychology* 50: 419–439.
Bumby, K.M., and Bumby, N.H. (1997). Adolescent female sexual offenders. In: *The Sex Offender: Volume II: New Insights, Treatment Innovations, and Legal Developments,* eds. B.K. Schwartz and H.R. Cellini, pp. 113–117. Kingston, NJ: Civic Research Institute.
Cath, A. H., Gurwitt, A. R., and Ross, J. M. (1982). eds. *Father and Child: Developmental and Clinical Perspectives.* Boston, MA: Little, Brown.
Cath, A. H., Gurwitt, A. R., and Gunsberg, L. (1989). eds. *Fathers and Their Families.* Hillsdale, NJ: Analytic Press.
Chen, G., and Gueta, K. (2016). Gender differences in child abuse and intergenerational transmission of crime and substance abuse among Israeli inmates. *Journal of Family Violence* 31: 735–746.
Chibnall, J.G., Wolf, A., and Duckro, P.N. (1998). A national survey of the sexual trauma experiences of Catholic nuns. *Review of Religious Research* 40: 142–162.
Chodorow, N.J. (2002). Prejudice exposed: On Stephen Mitchell's pioneering investigations of the psychoanalytic treatment and mistreatment of homosexuality. *Studies in Gender and Sexuality* 3: 61–72.
Christoffel, K.K., Scheidt, P.C., Agran, P.F., Kraus, J.F., McLoughlin, E., and Paulson, J.A. (1992). Standard definitions for childhood injury research: Excerpts of a conference report. *Pediatrics* 89: 1027–1034.

Cohler, J. (1987). Sex, love, and incest. *Contemporary Psychoanalysis* 23: 604–620.
Colarusso, C. (1990). The third individuation: The effect of biological parenthood on separation-individuation processes in adulthood. *Psychoanalytic Study of the Child* 45: 170–194.
Colarusso, C. (1992). *Child and Adult Development: A Psychoanalytic Introduction for Clinicians*. New York: Plenum.
Colarusso, C. (2010). *The Long Shadow of Child Sexual Abuse: Developmental Effects Across the Life Cycle.* Lanham, MD: Jason Aronson
Colarusso, C., and Nemiroff, R. (1981). *Adult Development: A New Dimension in Psychodynamic Theory and Practice. New York: Plenum.*
Corbett, K. (2009a). Little Hans: Masculinity foretold. *Psychoanalytic Quarterly* 78: 733–764.
Corbett, K. (2009b). *Boyhoods: Rethinking Masculinities*. New Haven, CT: Yale University Press.
Cortoni, F. (2015). What is so special about female sexual offenders? Introduction to the special issue on female sexual offenders. *Sexual Abuse: A Journal of Research and Treatment,* 27: 232–234.
Craven, S., Brown, S., and Gilchrist, E. (2006). Sexual grooming of children: Review of literature and theoretical considerations. *Journal of Sexual Aggression* 12: 287–299.
Crosson-Tower, C. (1997). *Exploring Child Welfare: A Practice Perspective*. Boston, MA: Pearson Education, 2004.
Dabbs, J.M., Jr., Ruback, R.B., Frady, R.I., Hopper, C.H., and Sgoutas, D.S. (1988). Saliva testosterone and criminal violence among women. *Personality and Individual Differences* 9: 269–275.
Danilova, M (2017) #MeToo movement hitting universities. *Philadelphia Inquirer*, 12/29/17, p. A4.
Dardis, C.M., Edwards, K.M., Kelley, E.L., and Gidycz, C.A. (2013). Dating violence perpetration: The predictive roles of maternally versus paternally perpetrated childhood abuse and subsequent dating violence attitudes and behaviors. *Journal of Aggression, Maltreatment & Trauma* 22: 6–25.
Davies, J.M. (1996). Dissociation, repression, and reality testing in the countertransference: The controversy over memory and false memory in the psychoanalytic treatment of adult survivors of childhood sexual abuse. *Psychoanalytic Dialogues* 6: 189–218.
De Bellis, M.D., Spratt, E.G., and Hooper, S.R. (2011). Neurodevelopmental biology associated with childhood sexual abuse. *Journal of Child Sexual Abuse* 20: 548–587.
DeCou, C.R., Cole, T.T., Rowland, S.E., Kaplan, S.P., and Lynch, S.M. (2015). An ecological process model of female sex offending: The role of victimization, psychological distress, and life stressors. *Sexual Abuse: A Journal of Research and Treatment* 27: 302–323.
Diaz, J. (2018). The silence. *The New Yorker*, pp. 11–17. April 16, 2018.
DiLillo, D., Tremblay, G., and Peterson, L. (2000). Maternal anger. *Child Abuse and Neglect* 24: 767–779.
Dimen, M. (2014). Both given and made: Commentary on Sakeopoulou. *Journal of the American Psychoanalytic Association* 62: 807–814.
Drescher, J. (2008). A history of homosexuality and organized psychoanalysis. *Journal of the American Academy of Psychoanalysis and Dynamic Psychiatry* 36: 443–460.
Duke, S.A., Balzer, B.W.R., and Steinbeck, K.S. (2014). Testosterone and its effects on human male adolescent mood and behavior: A systematic review. *Journal of Adolescent Health* 55: 315–322.
Dura-Vila, G., Littlewood, R., and Leavey, G. (2013). Integration of sexual trauma in a religious narrative: Transformation, resolution and growth among contemplative nuns. *Transcultural Psychiatry* 50: 21–46.
Ehlers, C.L., Rickler, K.C., Hovey, J.E. (1980). A possible relationship between plasma testosterone and aggressive behavior in a female outpatient population. In: *Limbic Epilepsy and Dyscontrol Syndrome*, eds. M. Girgis and L.G. Kiloh, pp. 68–91. New York: North Holland Biomedical Press.
Elise, D. (1997). Primary femininity, bisexuality, and the female ego ideal: A re-examination of female developmental theory. *Psychoanalytic Quarterly* 66: 489–517.

Elliott, M., Browne, K., and Kilcoyne, J. (1995). Child sexual abuse prevention: What offenders tell us. *Child Abuse and Neglect* 5: 579–594.
Erickson, E.H. (1963). *Childhood and Society*. New York: W.W. Norton.
Fairbairn, W.R.D. (1940). Schizoid factors in the personality. In: *An Object Relations Theory of Personality*, pp. 3–27. New York: Basic Books, 1952.
Fater, K., and Mullaney, J. A. (2000). The lived experience of adult male survivors who allege childhood sexual abuse by clergy. *Issues in Mental Health Nursing* 21: 281–295.
Farley, M. (2015). *prostitutionresearch.com*. Accessed October 20, 2017.
Fehr, E., Naef, M., Eisenegger, C., Snozzi, R., and Heinrichs, M. (2010). Prejudice and truth about the effect of testosterone on human bargaining behaviour. *Nature,* 463: 356–359.
Fernczi, S. (1932). *The Clinical Diary of Sandor Ferenczi*, transl. M. Balint and N. Jackson. Cambridge, MA: Harvard University Press, 1988.
Ferenczi, S. (1933). On the confusion of tongues between adults and the child. In: *Final Contributions to the Problems and Methods of Psychoanalysis,* pp. 155–167. New York: Basic Books, 1955.
Fernandez-Guasti, A., Kruijver, F.P.M., Fodor, M., and Swaab, D.R. (2000). Sex differences in the distribution of androgen receptors in the human hypothalamus. *Journal of Comparative Neurology* 425: 422–435.
Finkelhor, D., and Baron, L. (1986). Risk factors for child sexual abuse. *Journal of Interpersonal Violence* 1: 43–71.
Finkelhor, D., Ormrod, R.K., and Turner, H.A. (2010). Poly-victimization in a national sample of children and youth. *American Journal of Preventive Medicine* 38: 323–330.
Fischer R. (1991). The unresolved rapprochement crisis: An important constituent of the incest experience. In: *The Trauma of Transgression: The Psychotherapy of Incest Victims*, eds. S. Kramer, and S. Akhtar, pp. 39–56. Northvale, NJ: Jason Aronson Inc.
Fischer, R. (2015). Webinar: Human Trafficking: Training Healthcare. www.healthcareagainsttrafficking.com Accessed February 2018.
Fonagy, P. (2001). *Attachment Theory and Psychoanalysis*. New York: Other Press.
Fonagy, P., Gergely, G., Jursit, E., and Target, M. (2002) *Affect Regulation, Mentalisation and the Development of the Self.* New York: Other Press.
Fonagy, P., and Target, M. (1998). Mentalization and the changing aims of child psychoanalysis. *Psychoanalytic Dialogues* 8: 87–114.
Frank, A. (1969). Unrememberable and unforgettable: Passive primal repression. *Psychoanalytic Study of the Child* 22: 55–71.
Frank, E.R. (2015). *Dime*. New York: Simon and Shuster.
French, B.H., Tilghman, J.D., and Malebranche, D.A. (2015). Sexual coercion context and psychosocial correlates among diverse males. *Psychology of Men and Masculinity,* 16: 42–53.
Freud, A. (1946). *The Ego and the Mechanisms of Defense*. New York: International Universities Press.
Freud, S. (1893). The psychotherapy of hysteria from Studies on Hysteria. *Standard Edition* 2: 253–305.
Freud, S. (1895). Studies on hysteria (with Joseph Breuer). *Standard Edition 2*: 1–323.
Freud, S. (1896). The "specific" aetiology of hysteria. *Standard Edition 3*: 163–168.
Freud, S. (1900). The interpretation of dreams. *Standard Edition* 4–5.
Freud, S. (1912). On the universal tendency of debasement in the sphere of love. *Standard Edition* 11: 179–190.
Freud, S. (1914). On the history of the psycho-analytic movement. *Standard Edition* 14: 7–66.
Freud, S. (1916). Introductory lectures on psychoanalysis. *Standard Edition 16*: 243–463.
Freud, S. (1920). Beyond the pleasure principle. *Standard Edition* 18: 7–64.
Freud, S. (1923) The ego and the id. *Standard Edition* 19: 1–66.
Freud, S. (1933). New introductory lectures to psychoanalysis. *Standard Edition* 22: 7–182.
Freud, S. (1938). An outline of psychoanalysis. *Standard Edition* 23: 139–207.
Freud, S. (1940). An outline of psycho-analysis. *Standard Edition* 23: 139–207.
Furman, E. (1956). An ego disturbance in a young child. *Psychoanalytic Study of the Child* 11: 312–335.

Furman, E. (1985). On fusion, integration, and feeling good. *Psychoanalytic Study of the Child* 40: 81–110.
Furman, E. (1986). On trauma—when is the death of a parent traumatic? *Psychoanalytic Study of the Child* 41: 191–208.
Furman, E. (1998). Experiences in working with atypical children. *Child Analysis: Clinical, Theoretical, and Applied* 11: 138–155.
Gabbard, G. (1997). Challenges in the analysis of adult patients with histories of childhood sexual abuse. *Canadian Journal of Psychoanalysis* 5: 1–25.
Gabbard, G. (2016). *Boundary and Boundary Violations in Psychoanalysis, 2nd Edition*. Arlington, VA: American Psychiatric Association Publishing.
Gabbard, G.O., and Lester, E. (1995). *Boundaries and Boundary Violations in Psychoanalysis*. New York: Basic Books.
Gannon, T.A., and Rose, M.R. (2008). Female child sexual offenders: Toward integrating theory and practice. *Aggression and Violent Behavior* 13: 442–461.
Gannon, T.A., Rose, M.R., and Ward, T. (2008). A descriptive model of the offense process for female sexual offenders. *Sexual Abuse: A Journal of Research and Treatment* 20: 352–374.
Ganzarian, R.C., and Buchele, J. (1989). *Fugitives of Incest: A Perspective from Psychoanalysis and Group Psychotherapy*. Madison, CT: International Universities Press.
Gartner, R.B. (1997). *Daring to Remember: a Review of Memories of Sexual Betrayal: Truth, Fantasy, Depression, and Dissociation*. Northvale, NJ: Jason Aronson.
Ghetti, S., Edelstein, R.S., Goodman, G.S., Cordon, I.M., Quas, J.A., Alexander, K.W., and Jones, D.P. (2006). What can subjective forgetting tell us about memory for childhood trauma? *Memory and Cognition* 34: 1011–1025.
Glaser, R., and Dimitrakakis, C. (2013). Testosterone therapy in women: Myths and misconceptions. *Maturitas*, 74(3): 230–234.
Gilmore, K., and Meersand, P. (2014). *Normal Child and Adolescent Development: A Psychodynamic Primer*. Washington, DC, American Psychiatric Publishing.
Gomez-Gil, E., Zubiaurre-Elorza, L., Esteva, I., Guillamon, A., Godas, T., Almaraz, M.C. Halperin, I., and Salamero, M. (2012). Hormone-treated transsexuals report less social distress, anxiety and depression. *Psychoneuroendocrinology* 37: 662–670.
Goodman, G.S., Goldfarb, D., Quas, J.A., and Lyon, A. (2017). Psychological counseling and accuracy of memory for child sexual abuse. *American Psychologist* 72: 920-931.
Grand, S. (1997). The paradox of innocence: Dissociative "adhesive" states in perpetrators of incest. *Psychoanalytic Dialogues* 7: 465–490.
Grand, S. (2002). *The Reproduction of Evil: Clinical and Cultural Perspec*tive. Mahwah, NJ: Analytic Press.
Green, A. (1973). Le double et l'absent. *Critique* 3: 312–321.
Green, A. (1980). The dead mother. In: *Life Narcissism, Death Narcissism*, transl. A. Weller, pp. 185–221. London, UK: Free Association Books.
Greenacre, P. (1956). Re-evaluation of the process of working through. *International Journal of Psychoanalysis* 23: 439–444.
Harris, A. (2017). Women and activism: a long history, a complex problem. In: *The Status of Women: Violence, Identity, and Activism*, ed. V. Pender, pp. 237–252. London: Karnac Books.
Hay, D.F. (2007). The gradual emergence of sex differences in aggression: Alternative hypotheses. *Psychological Medicine* 37: 1527–1537.
Herman, J.L. (1992). *Trauma and Recovery—From Domestic Abuse to Political Terror*. New York: Basic Books.
Hetherton, J. (1999). The idealization of women: Its role in the minimization of child sexual abuse by females. *Child Abuse and Neglect* 23: 161–174.
Hines, M. (2004). *Brain Gender*. Oxford, UK: Oxford University Press.
Isely, P.J., Isely, P., Freiburger, J., and McMackin, R. (2008). In their own voices: A qualitative study of men abused as children by Catholic clergy. *Journal of Child Sexual Abuse* 17: 201–215.
Jones, M. (2018). What teenagers are learning from online porn. *New York Times Magazine*, pp. 10–14. February 7, 2018.

Katan, A. (1961). Some thoughts about the role of verbalization in early childhood. *Psychoanalytic Study of the Child* 16: 184–188.

Katan, A. (1973). Children who were raped. *Psychoanalytic Study of the Child* 28: 208–224.

Katz, M., Hampton, R.L., Newberger, E.H., Bowies, R.T., and Snyder, J.C. (1986). Returning children home: Clinical decision-making in cases of child abuse and neglect. *American Journal of Orthopsychiatry* 56: 253–262.

Kaufman, K., Holmberg, J.K, Orts, K.A., McCrady, F.E., Rotzien, A.L., Daleiden, E.L., and Hilliker, D.R. (1998). Factors influencing sexual offenders' modus operandi: An examination of victim-offender relatedness and age. *Child Maltreatment* 3: 349–361.

Kaufman, K., and Patterson, L. (2010). Using sex offenders' modus operandi to plan more effective prevention programs. In: *The Prevention of Sexual Violence: A Practitioner's Sourcebook*, ed. K. Kaufman, pp. 331–344. Holyoke, MA: NEARI Press.

Kempe, C.H., Silverman, N., Steele, B.F., Droegemueller, H., and Silver, H. (1962). The battered child syndrome. *Journal of the American Medical Association* 181:17–24.

Kenny, M.C., and McEachern, A.G. (2000). Racial, ethnic, and cultural factors of childhood sexual abuse: A selected review of the literature. *Clinical Psychology Review* 20: 905–922.

Khan, M. (1963). The concept of cumulative trauma. *Psychoanalytic Study of the Child* 18: 286.

Khan, M. (1983). *Hidden Selves: Between Theory and Practice in Psychoanalysis.* New York: International University Press.

Kilpatrick, A.C., and Holland, T.P. (1999). *Working with Families: An Integrative Model by Level of Need.* Needham Heights, MA: Allyn and Bacon.

King, M.L., Jr. (1958). Out of the long night. *The Gospel Messenger*, February 8, 1958, p. 14.

Kleinschmidt, L. (2009). Keeping mother alive: Psychotherapy with a teenage mother following human trafficking. *Journal of Child Psychotherapy.* 35: 262–275.

Kluft, R. (1990). *Incest-Related Syndromes of Adult Psychopathology.* Washington, DC: American Psychiatric Press, In.

Kohut, H. (1971). Analysis of the Self. New York: International University Press.

Kohut, H. (1977). *The Restoration of the Self.* New York: International Universities Press.

Korner, A. (1973). Sex differences in newborns with special references to differences in organization of oral behavior. *Journal of Child Psychology and Psychiatry* 14: 18–29.

Kramer, S. (1983). Object coercive doubting: A pathological defensive response to maternal incest. *Journal of the Psychoanalytic Association* 31S: 325–351.

Kramer, S. (1990). Residues of incest. In: *Adult Analysis and Childhood Sexual Abuse*, ed. H. Levine, pp. 149–170. Hillsdale, NJ: Analytic Press.

Kramer, S. (1991). Psychopathological effects of incest. In: *The Trauma of Transgression: Psychotherapy of Incest Victims.* eds. S. Kramer and S. Akhtar, pp. 1–12. Northvale, NJ: Jason Aronson.

Kramer S., and Akhtar S. (1991). eds. The Trauma of Transgression: Psychotherapy of Incest Victims. Northvale, NJ: Jason Aronson.

Krystal, H. (1978). Trauma and affects. *Psychoanalytic Study of the Child* 33: 81–116.

Laplanche, J., and Pontalis, J.B. (1973). *The Language of Psychoanalysis.* transl. D. Nicholson-Smith. New York: W.W. Norton.

Levenson, J., and Morin, J. (2001). *Treating Non-offending Parents in Child Sexual Abuse Cases.* Thousand Oaks, CA: Sage Publications Inc.

Levine, H. (1990). ed. *Adult Analysis and Childhood Sexual Abuse.* Hillsdale, NJ: Analytic Press.

Lieberman, A. F., Chu, A., Van Horn, P., and Harris, W. M. (2011). Trauma in early childhood: Empirical evidence and clinical implications. *Development and Psychopathology* 23: 397–410.

Liberman, A. F., Ghosh Ippen, C., and Van Horn, P. (2015). *"Don't Hit My Mommy!" A Manual for Child-Parent Psychotherapy with Young Children Exposed to Violence and Other Trauma (2nd edition).* Washington, DC: Zero to Three.

Loftus, E.F. (1993). Reality of repressed memory. *American Psychologist* 48: 518–537.

Lynn, S.J., Lock, T., Loftus, E.F., Krackow, E., and Lilienfeld, S.O. (2003). The remembrance of things past: Problematic memory recovery techniques in psychotherapy. In: *Science and*

Pseudoscience in Clinical Psychology, eds. S.O. Lilienfeld, S.J. Lynn, and J.M. Lohr, pp. 205–239. New York: Guilford Press.
MacKenzie, M.J., Kotch, J.B., and Lee, L. (2011). Toward a cumulative ecological risk model for the etiology of child maltreatment. *Children and Youth Services Review* 33: 1638–1647.
Mahler, M.S. (1972). Rapprochement subphase of the separation-individuation process. *Psychoanalytic Quarterly* 41: 487–506.
Mahler, M., Pine, F., and Bergman, A. (1975). *The Psychological Birth of the Human Infant.* New York: Basic Books.
Malarek, V. (2011). *The Johns: Sex for Sale and the Men Who Buy It.* New York: Arcade Publishing.
Margolis, M. (1991). Parent-child incest: Analytic treatment experiences with follow-up data. In: *The Trauma of Transgression*. eds. S. Kramer and S. Akhtar, pp. 55–91. Northvale, NJ: Jason Aronson.
Masson, J. (1984). The Assault on Truth. New York: Penguin Books.
Mathews, R., Hunter, J.A., and Vuz, J. (1997). Juvenile female sex offenders: Clinical characteristics and treatment issues. *Sexual Abuse: A Journal of Research and Treatment* 9: 187–199.
Mayer, E.L. (1991). Towers and enclosed spaces: A preliminary report on gender differences in children's reactions to block structures. *Psychoanalytic Inquiry* 11: 480–510.
Mbagaya, C.V. (2010). *Child Maltreatment in Kenia, Zambia and the Netherlands: A Cross-cultural Comparison of Prevalence, Psycho-pathological Sequelae, and Mediation by PTSS.* Leiden, Netherlands: Drukkerij Mostert.
McAlinden, A. M. (2012). *"Grooming" and the Sexual Abuse of Children: Institutional, Internet, and Familial Dimensions*. Clarendon Series in Criminology. Oxford, UK: Oxford University Press.
McDonald, P., and Charlesworth, S. (2015). Workplace sexual harassment at the margins. *Work, Employment and Society* 30: 118–134.
McNally, R.J. (2005). *Remembering Trauma*. Cambridge, MA: Harvard University Press.
Medical Dictionary (2015) *https://medical-dictionary.thefreedictionary.com/informed+consent.* Accessed February, 2018.
Mepham, S. (2010). Disabled children: The right to feel safe. *Child Care in Practice* 16:19–34.
Moran, R. (2013). *Paid For: My Journey Through Prostitution.* New York: W.W. Norton.
Moulden, H.M., Firestone, P., Kingston, D.A., and Wexler, A.F. (2010). A description of sexual offending committed by Canadian teachers. *Journal of Child Sexual Abuse* 19: 403–418.
Nachmani, G. (1995). Trauma and ignorance. *Contemporary Psychoanalysis* 31: 423–450.
Nadel, L., Campbell, J., and Ryan, L. (2007). Autobiographical memory retrieval and hippocampal activation as a function of repetition and the passage of time. *Neural Plasticity* 2007: 1–14.
National Hotline Trafficking Resource Center *https://humantraffickinghotline.org/*. Accessed February 6, 2018.
New York Times: *https://www.nytimes.com/2018/02/07/magazine/teenagers-learning-online-porn-literacy-sex-education.html.* Accessed March 2018.
Ney, P. (1992). Transgenerational triangles of abuse: A model of family violence. In: *Violence: Interdisciplinary Perspectives*, ed. V. Viano, pp.15–25. New York: Hemisphere Publishing.
O'Connor, D.B., Archer, J., and Wu, F.C.W. (2004). Effects of testosterone on mood, aggression, and sexual behavior in young men: A double-blind, placebo-controlled, cross-over study. *Journal of Clinical Endocrinology Metabolism* 89: 2837–2845.
Olesker, W. (1990). Sex differences during the early separation-individuation process: Implications for gender identity formation. Journal of the American Psychoanalytic Association 38: 325–346.
Oliver, B.E. (2007). Preventing female-perpetrated sexual abuse. *Trauma, Violence, and Abuse* 8: 19–32.
Orange, D. (2017). The waning of ego and agency: Commentary on Togashi's "Being Thrown Into the World Without Informed Consent". *Psychoanalytic Self* 12: 35–39.

Parens, H. (1990). On the girl's psychosexual development: reconsiderations suggested from direct observation. *Journal of the American Psychoanalytic Association* 38: 743–770.
Parens, H. (2011). *Handling Children's Aggression Constructively: Toward Taming Human Destructiveness.* Lanhamm MD: Jason Aronson.
Pender, V. (2016). ed. *The Status of Women: Violence, Identity and Activism.* London: Karnac.
Pender, V. (2017). Human sex trafficking: Extreme violence against women and children. In: *The Courage to Fight Violence against Women*, eds. P. Ellman and N. Goodman, pp. 17–28. London : Karnac Books.
Person, E.S., and Klar, H. (1994). Establishing trauma: The difficulty distinguishing between memories and fantasies. *Journal of the American Psychoanalytic Association* 42: 1055–1081.
Peter, T. (2008). Speaking about the unspeakable: Exploring the impact of mother-daughter sexual abuse. *Violence Against Women* 14: 1033–1053.
Pinker, S. (2011). *The Better Angels of Our Nature*. New York: Viking Press
Pope, H.G. Jr., Kouri, E.M., and Hudson, J.I. (2000). Effects of supraphysiological doses of testosterone on mood and aggression in normal men. *Archives of General Psychiatry* 57: 133–140.
Potegal, M., and Archer, J. (2004). Sex differences in childhood anger and aggression. *Child and Adolescent Psychiatric Clinics of North America* 13: 513–528.
Pynoos, R.S. (1990). Post-traumatic stress in children and adolescents. In: *Psychiatric Disorders in Children and Adolescents,* eds. B. Garfinkel, G. Carlson, and E. Weller, pp. 48–63. Philadelphia, PA: Saunders.
Pynoos, R.S. (1993). Traumatic stress and developmental psychopathology in children and adolescents. In: *American Psychiatric Press review of Psychiatry, Vol. 12,* eds. J. Oldham, M. Riba, and A. Tasman, pp. 205–238. Washington, DC: American Psychiatric Press.
Palmer, S., Brown, R., Rae-Grant, N., Loughlin, M. (1999). Responding to children's disclosure of familial abuse: what survivors tells us. *Child Welfare* 78: 259–282.
Pine, F. (1987). *Developmental Theory and Clinical Process*. New Haven, CT: Yale University Press.
Pine, F. (1997). *Diversity and Direction in Psychoanalytic Technique*. New Haven, CT: Yale University Press.
Principe, G. F., and Schindewolf, E. (2012). Natural conversations as a source of false memories in children: Implications for the testimony of young witnesses. *Developmental Review* 32: 205–223.
Putnam, F.W. (1991). The satanic ritual abuse controversy. *Child Abuse and Neglect* 15: 175–179.
Raphling, D. (1994). A patient who was not sexually abused. In: *Journal of the American Psychoanalytic Association* 42:65–78.
Reiter, S., Bryan, D.N., and Shachar, I. (2007). Adolescents with intellectual disabilities as victims of abuse. *Journal of Intellectual Disabilities* 11: 371–387.
Rosen, I. (1993). Relational masochism: The search for a bad enough object. *Presented to the Topeka Psychoanalytic Society.*
Sarnoff, C. (1971). The ego structure of latency. *Psychoanalytic Quarterly* 40: 387–414.
Schiller, B-M. (2012). Representing female desire within a labial framework of sexuality. *Journal of the American Psychoanalytic Association* 60: 1161–1197.
Schore, A.N. (2001). The effects of early relational trauma on right brain development, affect regulation, and infant mental health. *Infant Mental Health Journal* 22: 201–269.
Sedlak, A.J., Mettenburg, J., Basena, M., Petta, I., McPherson, K., Greene, A., and Li, S. (2010). *Fourth National Incidence Study of Child Abuse and Neglect (NIS–4): Report to Congress, Executive Summary*. Washington, DC: U.S. Department of Health and Human Services, Administration for Children and Families.
Shakeshaft, C. (2004). Education sexual misconduct: A synthesis of existing literature. *USA Department of Education*, Document 2004–2009.
Shengold, L. (1963). The parent as Sphinx. *Journal of the American Psychoanalytic Association* 11: 725–751.

Shengold, L. (1979). Child abuse and deprivation: Soul murder. *Journal of the American Psychoanalytic Association* 27: 533–559.
Shengold, L (1989). *Soul Murder: The Effects of Childhood Abuse and Deprivation.* New Haven, CT: Yale University Press.
Shengold, L. (1999). *Soul Murder Revisited: Thoughts about Therapy, Hate, Love, and Memory.* New Haven, CT: Yale University Press.
Sherwin, B.B., and Gelfand, M.M. (1985). Sex steroids and affect in the surgical menopause: A double-blind, cross-over study. *Psychoneuroendocrinol*ogy 10: 325–335.
Silverman, S. (2015). The colonized mind: Gender, trauma, and mentalization. *Psychoanalytic Dialogues* 25: 51–66.
Simon, B. (1992) Incest: The history of an error in psychoanalysis. *Journal of the American Psychoanalytic Association* 40: 955–988.
Simon, B., and Bullock, C. (1994). Incest and psychoanalysis: Are we ready to fully acknowledge, bear, and understand? *Journal of the American Psychoanalytic Association* 42: 1261–-1281.
Sletvold, J. (2014). *The Embodied Psychoanalyst: From Freud to Reich to Relationality.* London: Routledge.
Smith, M., and Pazder, L. (1980). *Michelle Remembers.* New York: Pocket Books.
Snyder, H. N. (2000). *Sexual Assault of Young Children as Reported to Law Enforcement: Victim, Incident, and Offender Characteristics.* Washington, DC: U.S. Department of Justice, Office of Justice Programs, Bureau of Justice Statistics. Retrieved January 6, 2018 from www.bjs.gov/content/pub.
Spence, D. P. (1982). *Narrative Truth and Historical Truth.* New York: W.W. Norton.
Stemple, L., Flores, A., and Meyer, I.H. (2017). Sexual victimization perpetrated by women: Federal data reveal surprising prevalence. *Aggression and Violent Behavior* 34: 302–311.
Struckman-Johnson, C., Struckman-Johnson,D., and Anderson, P. (2003). Tactics of sexual coercion: When men and women won't take no for an answer. *Journal of Sex Research* 40: 76–86.
Su, T.P., Pagliaro, M., Schmidt, P.J., Pickar, D., Wolkowitz, O., and Rubinow, D.R. (1993). Neuropsychiatric effects of anabolic sterioids in male normal volunteers. *Journal of the American Medical Association* 269: 2760–2764.
Sullivan, J., Beech, A.R., Craig, L.A., and Gannon, T.A. (2010). Comparing intra-familial and extrafamilial child sexual abusers with professionals who have sexually abused children with whom they work. *International Journal of Offender Therapy and Comparative Criminology* 55: 56–74.
Summit, R.C. (1983). The child sexual abuse accommodation syndrome. *Child Abuse and Neglect* 7: 177–193.
Terr, L. (1990). *Too Scared to Cry: Psychic Trauma in Childhood.* New York: Basic Books.
Terr, L. (1991). Childhood traumas: An outline and overview. *American Journal of Psychiatry,* 148: 10–20.
Terry, K., and Freilich, J. (2012). Understanding child sexual abuse by Catholic priests from a situational perspective. *Journal of Child Sexual Abuse* 21: 437–455.
Tesone, J. (2003). *Incest(s) and the negation of otherness.* Ravello: IPA-COWAP.
Tesone, J. (2005). *Incest: The Stolen Body.* Lisbon: IPA-COWAP.
Travers, N. (2006). A brief examination of pedophilia and sexual abuse committed by nuns within the Catholic Church. *William and Mary Journal of Women and the Law* 12: 761–778.
Tricked: The Documentary (2013). Directed by J. Wasson and J. Wells. Produced by C. Ljungberg and J. Wells.
Tricker, R., Casaburi, R., Storer, T.W., Clevenger, B., Berman, N., Shirazi, A., and Bhasin, S. (1996). The effect of supraphysiological doses of testosterone on angry behavior in healthy eugonadal men—a clinical research center study. *Journal of Clinical Endocrinology Metabolism* 81: 3754–3758.
Tronick, E. (2007). *The Neurobehavioral and Social-Emotional Development of Infants and Children.* New York: W.W. Norton.
Tronick, E., and Cohn, J. (1989). Infant-mother face-to-face interaction: Age and gender differences in coordination and the occurrence of miscoordination. *Child Development* 60: 85–92.

Turner, D., and Briken, P. (2015). Child sexual abusers working with children-characteristics and risk factors. *Sexual Offender Treatment* 10. www.sexual-offendertreatment.org, accessed January 6, 2018.

Turner, D., Rettenberger, M., Yoon, D., Klein, V., Eher, R., and Briken, P. (2016). Risk assessment in child sexual abusers working with children. *Sexual Abuse: A Journal of Research and Treatment* 28: 572–596.

Tylim I. (2017). Machismo and the limits of male heterosexuality. In: *The Status of Women; Violence, Identity, and Activism*, ed. V. Pender, pp. 221–236. London: Karnac Books.

United Nations Human Rights. Protocol to Prevent, Suppress and Punish Trafficking in Persons Especially Women and Children, Supplementing the United Nations Convention Against Transnational Organized Crime. 2000. *http://www.ohchr.org/EN/ProfessionalInterest/Pages/ProtocolTraffickingInPersons.*aspx. Accessed February 2018.

United Nations Office of the High Commissioner for Human Rights. *http://www.ohchr.org/EN/pages/home.aspx.* Accessed February 3, 2018.

U.S. Department of Health and Human Services, Administration for Children and Families, Administration on Children, Youth and Families, Children's Bureau. (2017). *Child Maltreatment 2016. www.acf.hhs.gov/programs*, accessed January 6, 2018.

U.S. Department of Health and Human Services. National Human Trafficking Resource Center/Polaris Project 2015 Statistics. National Human Trafficking Resource Center. *www.polarisproject.org,* accessed February3, 2018.

U.S. Department of Justice. *Characteristics of Suspected Human Trafficking Incidents, 2008-2010.* Office of Justice Programs, Bureau of Justice Statistics. *www.bjs.gov,* accessed February 6, 2018.

US Department of Justice and Facts (2018). *www.justice.gov,* accessed February 6, 2018.

US Human Trafficking Reporting System. *https://ojp.gov/newsroom, a*ccessed February 2018.

Valenti, J. (2016). What does a lifetime of leers do to us? *New York Times*, Sunday, June 5, 2016.

van Anders, S.M., Steiger, J., and Goldey, K.L. (2015). Effects of gendered behavior on testosterone in women and men. *Proceedings of the National Academy of Sciences* 112: 13805–13810.

van der Kolk, B. (1987). *Psychological Trauma.* Washington, DC: American Psychiatric Press.

van der Kolk, B. (1996). The body keeps score: Approaches to the psychobiology of post-traumatic stress disorder. In: *Traumatic stress: The effects of overwhelming experience on mind, body, and society, eds.* B.A. van der Kolk and A.C. McFarlane, pp. 214–241. New York: Guilford Press.

van der Kolk, B. (2014). *The Body Keeps Score: Brain, Mind, and Body in the Healing of Trauma.* New York: Penguin.

Van Der Pahlen, B., Lindman, R., Sarkola, T., Makisalo, H., and Eriksson, C.J.P. (2002). An exploratory study on self-evaluated aggression and androgens in women. *Aggressive Behavior* 28: 273–280.

Van Goozen S.H.M., Cohen-Kettenis, P.T., Gooren, L.J.G., Frijda, N.H., and Van de Poll, N.E. (1995). Gender differences in behaviour: Activating effects of cross-sex hormones. *Psychoneuroendocrinology* 20: 343–363.

Vandiver, D.M., and Kercher, G. (2004). Offender and victim characteristics of registered female sex offenders in Texas: A proposed typology of female sexual offenders. *Sexual Abuse: A Journal of Research and Treatment* 16: 121–137.

Viano, E.C. (2007). Clerical sexual predators: Impact and aftermath. *Rivista di Criminologia* 12: 25–38.

Vingerhoets, A., and Scheirs, J. (2000). Sex differences in crying: Empirical findings and possible explanations. In: *Gender and Emotion*, ed. A.H. Fischer. Cambridge: Cambridge University Press.

Weinberg, M., Tronick, E., Cohn, J., and Olson, K. (1999). Gender differences in emotional expressivity and self-regulation during early infancy. *Developmental Psychology* 35: 175–188.

Winnicott, D. (1956). Primary maternal preoccupation. In: *Collected Papers: Through Paediatrics to Psychoanalysis,* pp. 300–305. New York: Basic Books, 1958.

Wolfe, D.A. (1994). The role of intervention and treatment services in the prevention of child abuse and neglect. In: *Protecting Children from Abuse and Neglect: Foundations for a New Strategy*, eds. G.B. Melton and F.D. Barry, pp. 224–303. New York: Guilford Press.

World Health Organization. (2015). *http://www.who.int/gho/en/*. Accessed February 2, 2018.

Wurtele, S.K., Simons, D.A., and Moreno, T. (2014). Sexual interest in children among an online sample of men and women: Prevalence and correlates. *Sexual Abuse: A Journal of Research and Treatment* 26: 546–568.

Yates, W.R., Perry, P.J., MacIndoe, J., Holman, T., and Ellingrod, V. (1999). Psychosexual effects of three doses of testosterone cycling in normal men. *Biol Psychiat,* 45: 254–260.

Young-Bruehl, E. (2010). Sexual diversity in cosmopolitan perspective. *Studies in Gender and Sexuality* 11: 1–9.

Young-Bruehl, E. (2012). *Childism*. New Haven, CT: Yale University Press.

Zastrow, C.H., and Kirst-Ashman, K.K. (2004). *Understanding Human Behavior and the Social Environment*. Belmont, CA: Brooks/Cole.

Index

About the Editor and Contributors

Salman Akhtar, MD, professor of psychiatry, Jefferson Medical College; training and supervising analyst, Psychoanalytic Center of Philadelphia, Philadelphia, PA.

Thomas Barrett, PhD, former chairman and current adjunct professor of clinical psychology, Chicago School of Professional Psychology; private practice of psychotherapy and psychoanalysis, Chicago, IL.

Shawn Blue, PhD, assistant professor, Sidney Kimmel Medical College; psychologist, Student Personal Counseling Center, Department of Psychiatry and Human Behavior, Thomas Jefferson University, Philadelphia, PA.

Gordon Caras, PhD, faculty member, San Diego Center for Psychoanalysis; private practice of adult and child psychotherapy and psychoanalysis, Solana Beach, CA.

Calvin Colarusso, MD, clinical professor of psychiatry, University of California at San Diego; training and supervising analyst, San Diego Center for Psychoanalysis, San Diego, CA.

John Frank, MD, clinical professor of psychiatry, Drexel University School of Medicine; faculty member, Psychoanalytic Center of Philadelphia, Philadelphia, PA.

Christie Huddleston, MD, faculty member, Psychoanalytic Center of Philadelphia, Philadelphia, PA.

Vivian Pender, MD, clinical associate professor of psychiatry, Weill Cornell Medical College, New York; training and supervising analyst, Center for Psychoanalytic Training and Research, Columbia University, New York, NY.

Andrew Smolar, MD, assistant clinical professor of psychiatry, Drexel University School of Medicine; training and supervising analyst, Psychoanalytic Center of Philadelphia, Philadelphia, PA.

Ann G Smolen, PhD, training and supervising analyst, Psychoanalytic Center of Philadelphia, Philadelphia, PA.

www.ingramcontent.com/pod-product-compliance
Ingram Content Group UK Ltd.
Pitfield, Milton Keynes, MK11 3LW, UK
UKHW041123071026
15587UKWH00009B/103

9 781498 587839